O R D E R I N G   I N F O R M A T I O N

Order your copy of *The Mechanics of Writing* from Amazon.com. To receive a discount on bulk orders, go to www.wtkpublishing.com.

The Mechanics of Writing

Which Comes First, the Comma or the Pause?

Dona J. Young

The Mechanics of Writing

Dona J. Young

1st Edition—May 29, 2008

Copyright © Writer's Toolkit Publishing LLC

All rights reserved

www.wtkpublishing.com

ISBN: 978-0-9815742-2-6

Printed in the United States

Introduction

The Mechanics of Writing starts by posing a question common to most writers: *Which comes first, the comma or the pause?* Learning the answer to this basic question is the doorway to understanding punctuation as well as structure. Right now, let's cut to the chase and give you an answer you may not be expecting: *the comma comes first, the pause follows.*

That is the opposite of what the vast majority of writers believe, even good writers. If this news feels like a revelation to you, as it does to most, you can understand why some writing decisions are so confusing at times. In fact, other types of writing decisions may baffle you as well; for example, do you always know the difference between a fragment or a run-on and a complete sentence? Do you sometimes feel a bit nervous about your writing when someone such as a teacher or your boss will read it?

Learning comma rules, like most grammar topics, is like unrolling a ball of yarn. Principles of one topic are linked to principles of another topic—that is why it sometimes feels impossible to make progress. However, this book untangles that ball of yarn for you, helping you make decisions that lead to correct writing. As you learn each new principle, your editing skills will improve and, thus, the quality of your writing will also improve.

This little handbook, unlike other grammar handbooks, organizes the essential topics for you, ordering them so that learning makes sense. In other words, this book develops a string of concepts that builds from one to another. This approach simplifies learning the mechanics of writing, but it is up to you to apply what you are learning in your own writing.

That is why it is important to learn some basic principles about sentences before jumping right in and starting with comma rules. By the time you start working on comma rules in Lesson 4, the terminology will not sound overwhelming. In fact, the foundation that you are building will make writing easier for you for the rest of your career.

Start by taking the pretest at the end of Lesson 1. Your score will give you a starting point from which you can gauge your skill development. Work through each lesson, doing the activities as prescribed.

The keys to the exercises are included in this book so that you have immediate reinforcement for your practice. You will find the keys to the Skill Builder activities at the end of each lesson; however, the keys to the Skills

Workshop are located at the back of the book in **Keys to Assessments and Worksheets**.

Good luck on your journey to improving your writing skills. Practice makes progress: repetition is the key to learning any skill, including writing. *Now go for it!*

Dona Young

February 11, 2008

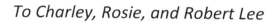
To Charley, Rosie, and Robert Lee

The Mechanics of Writing

This handbook covers major principles that lead to correct writing.

BRIEF CONTENTS

About This Book

The Mechanics of Writing was written to assist writers of all levels—students and professionals alike—gain control of their proofreading skills.

The subtitle of this book, *Which Comes First, the Comma or the Pause?*, has a broader meaning than you might expect: the word *pause* not only refers to decisions about commas, *pause* also symbolizes an approach to making writing decisions. Rather than basing decisions on solid principles, writers instead base many of their decisions on guesses or whims. That is partly because looking up every question in a reference manual can be time-consuming.

If the pause approach has not worked for you, try the systematic approach to building skills that this book presents. You will learn principles on which to base common writing decisions. Then you will practice those principles, applying what you are learning while the concepts are fresh.

Unlike most handbooks, this book is meant to be read from cover to cover. That is because it untangles grammar, building from one concept to another. Though it covers the basics, it covers them in a fast-paced and highly focused way. In fact, thousands of business professionals have used this approach to improve their writing, producing higher-quality writing in less time and with greater confidence.

As you work through each lesson of this book, you will steadily improve your proofreading and editing skills. Eventually, many writing decisions will become automatic: you will no longer rely on guessing but rather will rely on solid principles that lead you to achieve a higher standard. As your writing skills improve, so will your career opportunities.

Note: The student Web site for this book, www.commasrule.com, contains additional practice exercises.

CONTENTS

1

The Comma,
the *Pause*, and the Plan

Oscar Wilde illustrated the confusion surrounding commas and pauses perfectly when he said, "I have spent most of the day putting in a comma and the rest of the day taking it out."

At some point, you have probably found yourself in a similar situation: reading a sentence over and over again searching for the *right pause* and never quite being able to nail it down. For truth be known, commas do not depend on pauses, which is contrary to the most common understanding of how to place commas. Commas are correctly placed based on comma rules, and comma rules are based on structure and rooted in grammar.

Grammar takes the guessing out of where you can place all punctuation marks, and that includes the period, semicolon, colon, and dash as well as the comma. So remember: *the comma comes first, and the pause follows.*

As you learn more about structure, you will also more readily see the natural breaks in grammar, which are also natural places to take a breath or pause, especially when reading out loud. Here is the irony: once you can easily identify natural breaks in grammar, which will happen as a result of learning comma rules, the "right pauses" will suddenly become clear and identifiable at a glance.

However, decisions about commas can interfere with writing for another reason. For example, when you stop to figure out where to place a comma, do you ever lose your train of thought? Or maybe your ideas dissolve when you stop to find the "right word" or even the "right spelling" of the right word. Getting your words down "right" refocuses your attention away from developing your thoughts, interfering with your writing the same way as the "right pause" does.

Though commas can be frustrating, they are actually only a symptom of a broader issue: *basing writing decisions on guesses rather than principles.* In fact, any writing decision based on guessing can rob you of your energy and confidence. And let's face it, your primary reason for learning about commas is to improve your writing.

This book untangles the mechanics of writing. Rather than guessing, you will learn solid principles on which to base your writing decisions. With enough practice, many writing decisions will become automatic and, over time, the quality of your writing will improve.

However, before learning the mechanics of writing, you need to learn how to manage the writing process so that you can get your ideas on the page. You see, not knowing the *right word* or the *right pause* does not need to rob you of your ideas—when you lose your thoughts, it is because you are not managing the writing process effectively.

The Writing Process

By learning more about the writing process, you can immediately and dramatically improve some aspects of your writing. The writing process consists of distinct phases, for example:

- **Composing:** creating, inventing, exploring, solving problems
- **Proofreading:** correcting grammar, spelling, and punctuation
- **Editing:** improving the quality and structure of sentences
- **Revising:** changing the flow of ideas and, at times, the purpose

A major reason your words dissolve before they reach the page is that you may be doing everything at once, such as making proofreading or editing decisions while you compose.

If you find yourself editing as you compose, *stop immediately*. In other words, the time to figure out where to put in a comma is not while you are composing (or even revising). Build a wall between all composing activities and all forms of editing and proofreading. Make the following your motto:

Compose fearlessly, edit ruthlessly.

If you do not feel ready to compose, do any activity that helps you learn you topic in more depth. So let's add one more phase to the writing process, recognizing that the writing process begins *before* you begin to compose.

- **Pre-writing:** reading, thinking, discussing, summarizing

To develop your critical thinking, do pre-writing activities: summarize what you are learning as you go along, jotting down insights and questions.

You will become a better editor by learning comma rules. However, the only way you can become a better writer is to write more. Let's take a look at some painless ways of getting started and getting organized.

Writing Tools

Use the following techniques to manage the writing process so that you compose more fluently: mind mapping, freewriting, focused writing, and page mapping.

Mind mapping. This form of brainstorming allows you to get your ideas on the page in a quick, spontaneous way. First, choose your topic. Next, write your topic in a "bubble" in the middle of the page. Finally, free associate ideas and cluster them around your topic. Here is an example of mind mapping in response to the question, "What is difficult about writing?"

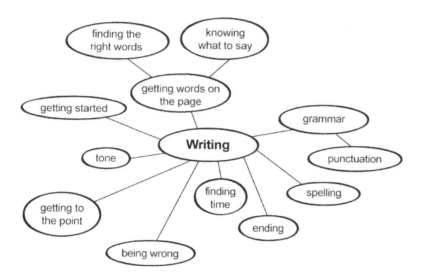

Scratch outline. Rather than using the clustering technique of mind mapping, simply make a list of your ideas as they pop into your mind.

Freewriting. Get your words down in a free flow, stream of consciousness way by picking up a pen and writing down your thoughts. This activity helps you build your ability to compose fearlessly while blocking out your compulsion to correct your writing.

If you have never tried freewriting, you owe it to yourself to try it. Some people set aside 10 minutes a day for releasing their thoughts on the page. It works. If you try it, you are likely to find yourself more clear-headed and focused. Since writing is a problem-solving activity, you may also find yourself actively working on solving problems that now drain your energy.

Focused writing. Choose a topic and write about only that topic for a specified amount of time, such as 10 to 15 minutes or 3 pages. Focused writing can help you make good use of small amounts of time that would otherwise be lost.

Page mapping. Put your main ideas or key points from your scratch outline or mind map along the side of a blank page. Then fill in the details by using each key point as the topic for a focused-writing activity. This technique helps eliminate one of the biggest fears of any writing task: starting with a blank page.

In each lesson, including this one, you will find a short activity which requires writing; some of the activities recommend using one or more of these tools to get started or get organized. If you have the time, select one or two that you have never tried and try them now.

The Plan

To maximize your results, follow the plan outlined here. In some ways it is foolproof, so do not second-guess yourself or cut corners.

1. *Before you start the next lesson, complete the assessment at the end of this lesson.*

Your score will give you a realistic idea of your current skill level, letting you know why writing decisions seem so difficult at times. However, your score will also provide a baseline so that you can take a similar assessment in Lesson 10 and then compare your results. Once you have both scores, you will be able to calculate your percentage of improvement, supporting your sense of accomplishment and confidence.

2. *After you take the assessment, start with* **Lesson 2: The Sentence**.

You may think that because you have been writing for as long as you can remember that you do not need to learn about the sentence. However, unless you can define what a sentence is off of the top of your head and be able to identify the core of every sentence you read or write, Lesson 2 has value for you.

3. *Complete the brief exercises that are interspersed throughout each lesson.*

After each principle, you will find a **Skill Builder**, which is a brief exercise that allows you to apply the new principle. After you complete each Skill Builder, check the key located at the end of the lesson to get immediate reinforcement for your answers. Some lessons also contain **Workshop Activities**, which give you an opportunity to discuss concepts with a peer.

4. *Complete the worksheets at the end of each lesson.*

At the end of each lesson is a **Skills Workshop**, which contains a series of worksheets to give you more practice and application. Complete each worksheet exactly as the directions prescribe. In fact, do the worksheets with a partner, if you can. You will find the answers to the worksheets in **Keys to Assessments and Worksheets** located at the back of the book.

5. *Take the time to do the writing activity in the* **Writing Workshop**.

After the **Recap**, each lesson contains a **Writing Workshop**. Each Writing Workshop provides activities designed to be somewhat self-reflective. They are included because working on writing mechanics is not meaningful unless you apply what you are learning through the writing process. In addition to giving you practice with writing tools such as mind mapping and focused writing, these activities help you learn to separate composing from editing.

6. *Keep a journal.*

Journaling can help you build your writing skills as you work on setting and achieving your goals. Follow the 2 x 4 method: write two pages on four different days each week. The Writing Workshop includes an activity that involves journaling.

Recap

Learning principles of mechanics and style can help you make more effective writing decisions with less effort. However, no one can teach you to write: writing comes from within. The only way to become a better writer is to write more, using writing as a problem-solving tool. Here are some of the key points stressed in this lesson:

> ➤ Commas are not placed based on pauses: comma rules determine where to place commas.

> ➤ The *pause* also represents other types of writing decisions that are based on guesses rather than solid principles.

> ➤ The way to improve your writing skills is to learn principles and practice them, eventually applying them in your own writing.

> ➤ With enough practice, writing decisions will become automatic.

> ➤ Manage the writing process by keeping all composing activities separate from editing: *Compose fearlessly, edit ruthlessly!*

> ➤ To get started and stay focused, use tools such as mind mapping, scratch outlines, focused writing, and page maps.

> ➤ Follow the plan outlined in this lesson—no excuses and no shortcuts!

Writing is a problem-solving activity. As you build your writing skills, you are also building your critical thinking skills, which will enhance your career and give you more opportunities.

Writing Workshop

Do the following activities to gain insight into your writing process:

A. Instructions: Write a brief paper defining what is difficult about writing.

1. Include what you think about your ability to write as well as experiences that may have shaped your feelings about writing.
2. Start by mind mapping the question or by completing a scratch outline.
3. Next, do a focused writing: write freely without editing your words.
4. Finally, put your rough draft in final form.
5. If you can, share your experiences with a partner, ending with what each of you finds beneficial about writing.

B. Instructions: Start your journal, and follow the 2 x 4 method.

1. Get a notebook for your journal so that you can stay organized.
2. Make your first journal entry: sit down and write for 10 minutes, pouring whatever is on your mind onto the pages of your journal. Do not worry about grammar, punctuation, or spelling: *just write!*
3. Commit yourself to writing about two pages at least four times a week.

Skills Workshop

Pre-Assessment

Complete the following assessment to gauge your current skills accurately. After you take this pre-assessment, tear it out and put it in a safe place so that you have it as a base of comparison. (Or you may choose to make a copy of the assessment rather than using the one in the book. At any rate, store your completed test in a safe place so that you have it when you finish the book.)

It's not about the test: It's about what you learn. Refrain from reviewing the pre-assessment until you complete the book. If you pay too much attention to how you did or start turning back and forth between the test and the new principles that you are learning, your final score will not be a true assessment of your improvement. Trust the process: you will improve!

Part A. Punctuation: Commas and Semicolons

Instructions: Place commas and semicolons where needed in the following sentences.

1. When you arrive in Tampa call our district manager.

2. Reserve March 15 2009 for our reception.

3. Boston Massachusetts is a great city for a conference.

4. McKenzie will manage the project however Bill will help.

5. As you go through life always attempt to solve problems in a positive way.

6. No one has all the answers but everyone has something to contribute.

7. Your presentation will be a success you know your topic well.

8. However you should still practice until you feel confident.

9. Martha thank you for giving me that advice.

10. I will help you with your plans if you wish.

11. Although I worked hard on the project I do not feel good about it.

12. My boss however said that it turned out well.

13. The time to act is now therefore give the interview your best.

14. They will make you the offer you have nothing to fear.

15. Bob my associate will be joining us for dinner.

Part B. Capitalization, Apostrophes, and Quotation Marks

Instructions: Make corrections in capitalization, apostrophes, and quotation marks as needed.

Last week i applied for a job and had to go to an Employment Interview. I was applying for a Managers position at a local restaurant. When i arrived, the Assistant Manager asked me, "do you live in the community"? Since i dont live nearby, i immediately thought that I would be out of the running for the position. I answered with a cheerful voice, "no, but I have access to good transportation". Before I left, the Owner needed to make a copy of my drivers license. Since my resume was missing my previous Employers contact information, I said that I would call back with the information.

Part C. Similar Words

Instructions: Correct word usage in the following sentences.

1. The principle and interest on your loan are due.

2. If the problem does not effect you, don't worry about it.

3. Ensure your manager that you will be on time.

4. The affect is not yet known.

5. Joe said that he would loan you his book.

6. The vehicle lost its' wheels.

7. All members of the committee should bring they're reports.

8. When you say its time to send in the report, we will.

9. Their working hard to solve the problem.

10. We all try to live by our principals.

Part D. Number Usage

1. Kenny ordered twelve notebooks, not five.

2. Are you available on September 10th for a meeting?

3. Jackson's current address is 1355 E. Archer.

4. When you say 1000s of people will be there, do you mean it?

5. The company sold two point five million dollars in products.

Note: You will find the key to the pretest and a score sheet in **Keys to Assessments and Worksheets**. However, it is advised that you wait to score the pretest until *after* you work through all ten lessons of this book and take the posttest. In that way, you will have an accurate assessment of how much your score improves based on skill development (rather than by becoming test savvy).

2

The Sentence

What does learning about the sentence have to do with commas and pauses? And what else can you learn about sentences that you do not already know?

- First, good writing depends as much on good editing as it does on good writers. The sentence is the base unit of editing: gain control of the sentence, and you gain control of your editing skills.

- Second, controlling the sentence depends on the ability to manipulate the sentence core. Do you currently feel skilled in achieving that?

This lesson and the next one provide principles to help you gain control of the sentence so that you can improve the quality and style of your writing. So do not take any short-cuts. Let's get started and learn about the sentence.

What Is a Sentence?

Think for a moment: *What is a sentence?* You have been writing sentences for a very long time, but can you define what a sentence is? Use the template below to write your own definition:

A sentence consists of a _____ and a _____ and expresses a _____ _____.

If you cannot fill in the template exactly, use the line below to jot down the words or ideas about sentences that pop into your mind.

_____

Once you can define what a sentence, you have reached the critical starting point of understanding grammar for writing.

Before reviewing the definition of what a sentence is, write a sentence or two below. (Feel free to compose sentences about anything that interests you—but keep them simple.)

Sentence 1: _____.

Sentence 2: _____.

Sentence 3: _____.

Here is the definition of a sentence:

> A **sentence** consists of a <u>subject</u> and a <u>verb</u> and expresses a <u>complete thought</u>.

Even if your definition does not match this definition exactly, it can still be correct. For example:

- Some people use the word *noun* instead of *subject*.
- Some use the word *predicate* instead of *verb*.
- Some use the phrase *can stand on its own*, rather than *complete thought*.

Another term for *sentence* is *independent clause*. The word *clause* refers to *a group of words that has a subject and verb*. When a clause cannot stand on its own, it is a *dependent clause*. Here is a recap:

- **Independent Clause**: a group of words that has a subject and verb and expresses a complete thought; an independent clause is a complete sentence.
- **Dependent Clause**: a group of words that has a subject and verb but does not express a complete thought; a dependent clause cannot stand on its own.

When a sentence consists of an independent clause and a dependent clause, the independent clause is the **main clause**.

Workshop Activity

Instructions: Before going on to a new concept, go back to the sentences you wrote on the previous page. If you can, work with a partner as you answer the following questions:

1. How did your definition of a sentence compare with the standard definition?

2. Can you pick out the subject and verb of each of the sentences that you wrote?

3. Read your sentences out loud—does each one express a complete thought?

As you read your sentences, notice if the question *What?* pops into your mind. If it does, you may have written a sentence **fragment** instead of a complete sentence. A fragment is a group of words that is punctuated as a sentence, but it is not a complete sentence. You will do more work with dependent clauses and fragments in Lesson 2.

What Is a Subject?

The subject of a sentence drives the action of the verb. Thus, the subject of a sentence answers the question *who?* or *what?* as in *who* or *what performs the action of the verb?* As Karen Gordon explains in *The Deluxe Transitive Vampire*, "the subject is that part of a sentence about which something is divulged; it is what the sentence's other words are gossiping about."[1]

The subject of a sentence usually comes in the form of a **noun** or a **pronoun** or a **phrase:**

- A noun is a person, place, or thing, but a noun can also be an intangible item that cannot be seen or felt, such as *joy* or *wind* or *integrity.*

- A pronoun is a word that can be used in place of a noun, such as *I, you, he, she, it, we, they, who,* and *someone,* among others.

- A phrase is a group of related words that does not have a subject *and* predicate and cannot stand alone.

A **complete subject** consists of the **simple subject** and all the words that modify it. For writing purposes, the simple subject is important for a few reasons, but primarily because the simple subject must agree with its verb. In the following, the simple subject of each sentence is underlined once:

My good <u>friend</u> assisted me with the writing task.

The new <u>manager</u> will chair the committee.

All <u>members</u> of the task force are in the conference room.

<u>They</u> are working diligently.

Her <u>honesty</u> is admirable.

All sentences have a **grammatical subject**: a grammatical subject is *the simple subject that precedes the verb in a statement*. Being able to recognize the grammatical subject is important; however, it is not always stated in the sentence. The grammatical subject is simply referred to as the "subject."

When the grammatical subject is not stated, it becomes an **implied subject**. Implied subjects come in the form of "you understood" or "I understood." Here is a recap:

- A grammatical subject precedes its verb in a statement.

- When the grammatical subject is not present in the sentence, it becomes an implied subject.

- Implied subjects come in the form of *you understood* or *I understood.*

- *You understood* is displayed as follows: (You).

- *I understood* is displayed as follows: (I).

In each of the following examples, the implied subject is in parentheses and the verb is double underscored:

(You) Please <u>take</u> your seat in the front of the room.

(You) <u>Feel</u> free to call me if you have a question.

(I) <u>Thank</u> you for your assistance.

Now let's learn a few details about verbs, but just enough to help you recognize them.

What Is a Verb?

Central to every sentence, **verbs** are words that express action or state of being. Here are few details to help you identify verbs:

- All verbs have a **base form**; *to* plus the base form of a verb is its **infinitive**: *to go, to see*.
- Most verbs express action, such as *go, walk, work,* and *finish*.
- A few verbs do not express action but instead express **state of being**. These **linking verbs** include *be, seem,* and *appear* and at times *feel, grow, act, look, smell, taste,* and *sound*.[2]
- All verbs have a **gerund form**: a gerund consists of *ing* plus the base form of the verb: *going, walking, being*.
- The verb is the only part of speech that changes time: past, present, and future.
- Verbs often string together, most often showing up in pairs (as in *will go* or *does know*).
- Common helping verbs are *to be* (is, are, was, were), *to have* (has, have, had), and *to do* (do, did, done).

Here are some hints to help you recognize the verb of a sentence:

1. Look for a word that expresses action, such as *speak, stop, implement,* or *recognize*.

2. Look for a word that tells time and in doing so changes form, such as *speak, spoke, spoken,* and so on.

3. Look for the words *not* and *will*:

   a. You will generally find a verb after the word *will,* such as *will implement, will speak, will recognize, will find,* and so on.

   b. You will generally find a verb before and after the word *not,** such as *did* not *go, has* not *recognized, has* not *implemented, has* not *spoken,* and so on.

***Note:** The word *not* does not function as a verb; instead, *not* modifies a verb and negates it.

Here are a few more examples:

Expressing Action:

Michael *finishes* his projects on time.

The committee *meets* every Friday.

I *complete* the inventory monthly.

Changing Time:

Michael *finished* his projects on time.

The committee *met* every Friday.

I *will complete* the inventory.

Preceding/Following *Not* or *Will*:

Michael *will finish* his projects on time.

The committee *did* not *meet* every Friday.

I *will* not *complete* the inventory.

In the following, the verb of each sentence is underlined twice, the subject once:

Alexander watched the PowerPoint presentation.

My new manager will apply the policy to everyone in our department.

The meeting is not scheduled for May 29.

He discovers errors in our reports every week.

At times, a verb will need a helper, which is also known as an **auxiliary**. When you see a helper verb, look for another verb to follow it. Here are common helping verbs and their various forms:

Infinitive	Verb Forms
to be	is, are, was, were, being
to have	have, has, had, having
to do	do, did, done, doing

In the following examples, verbs are underlined twice and subjects once:

Marc had offered to prepare the agenda.

The meeting was cancelled.

The change did not affect our schedules.

Workshop Activity

Instructions: Work with a partner on the following:

A. Go back to the sentences you wrote on page 12. Did you correctly identify the verb and subject of each sentence?

B. What is a grammatical subject? What is an implied subject?

What Is the Sentence Core?

Together the subject and verb form the **sentence core**. Being able to identify and control the core of a sentence will give you control of your grammar and, eventually, your writing style. Here are few points about subjects and verbs:

- In sentences, the subject almost always precedes the verb.

- The verb determines the subject of the sentence.

- The verb also determines the object, if there is one.

Here is a point about writing style: the closer the subject and verb are to each other, the easier it is for a reader to understand your writing. That is because the subject and verb together create meaning: without one or the other, the reader is lost. In other words, you will understand your meaning when you write a fragment; but until both the subject and verb are stated, clear meaning is *not* conveyed to your reader.

Statements are generally structured as subject – verb – object (S – V - O). In the following examples, the <u>verbs</u> are underlined twice; the <u>subjects</u>, once; and the **objects** are in bold typeface; for example:

<u>Marcus</u> <u>attended</u> the **conference**.
    S   V   O

While all sentences have a subject and verb, not all sentences have an object:

The <u>train</u> <u>arrived</u>.
     S   V

For questions, the subject and verb are partially inverted and a helper is needed:

<u>Did</u> the <u>train</u> <u>arrive</u>?
V   S   V

<u>Has</u> <u>Marcus</u> <u>attended</u> the **conference**?
V   S   V   O

It is easier to identify the subject and verb of a question if you first invert it back to a statement; for example:

The <u>train</u> <u>did</u> <u>arrive</u>.

<u>Marcus</u> <u>has</u> <u>attended</u> the conference.

In practice exercises, you will be asked to identify the verb first for the following two reasons:

1. The verb is easier to identify than the subject.

2. The verb of a sentence determines its subject.

After you identify the verb, you will work backward in the sentence to find its subject. (Note: You will *not* be asked to identify objects because the object is not a critical part of the sentence core.)

What Is a Compound Subject?

A compound subject consists or two or more words or phrases. Once again, you will be looking for the simple subject, but this time the simple subject will be "multiplied."

<u>Alice</u> and <u>Joyce</u> <u>attended</u> the reunion.

Your <u>brother</u> and <u>sister</u> <u>can</u> <u>assist</u> you with the family reunion.

My <u>manager</u> and the <u>vice president</u> <u>will</u> <u>decide</u> the dress code.

What Is a Compound Verb?

A compound verb is similar to a compound subject: you are looking for the simple verb, but there will be two or more main verbs along with their helpers, as in the following:

My <u>associate</u> <u>had</u> <u>called</u> and <u>asked</u> me for a favor.

Hard <u>work</u> <u>causes</u> me to apply myself and <u>focuses</u> my attention.

<u>Jogging</u> <u>improves</u> my health, <u>motivates</u> me, and <u>encourages</u> me to eat less.

A sentence can have both a compound subject and a compound verb, for example:

<u>Margie</u> and <u>Seth</u> <u>opened</u> the invitation and <u>expressed</u> their surprise.

Sentences that have compound verbs and compound subjects are different from compound sentences. Let's take a look at compound sentences so that you can see the difference.

What Is a Compound Sentence?

A compound sentence is a sentence that contains two main clauses. In other words, it is *two sentences rolled into one*!

<u>Joe</u> <u>called</u> about the opening in marketing, and <u>he</u> <u>expressed</u> an interest.

The new <u>ad</u> <u>will</u> <u>run</u> for two weeks, and then <u>we</u> <u>will</u> <u>need</u> a new one.

My <u>professor</u> <u>asked</u> me to give a presentation, and <u>I</u> <u>was</u> honored.

In the next lesson, you will learn about comma signals, but you will also learn more about clauses and fragments. Work on the exercises at the end of this lesson to gain practice applying what you have learned. Focused practice ensures that you build a solid foundation in your new skills.

Recap

This lesson has focused on sentence structure and the sentence core, which consists of the verb and its subject.

> ➢ To identify the sentence core of a statement, identify the verb first and then work backward to find its subject.

> ➢ To identify a verb, look for a word that expresses action or state of being and that changes form when it changes time (past, present, or future).

> ➢ To identify the sentence core of a question, first invert the question back to a statement and then identify the verb and its subject:

>> Are you going to the store? <u>You</u> <u>are</u> <u>going</u> to the store.

> ➢ Subjects can be implied or understood, such as *I understood* (I) or *You understood* (You):

>> (I) <u>Thank</u> you for your help or (You) <u>Take</u> your time.

> ➢ Verbs as well as subjects can be compound, which means that there is more than one.

>> <u>John</u> and <u>Bryan</u> <u>will</u> <u>assist</u> us and <u>give</u> us their best advice.

> ➢ Compound sentences have more than one main clause.

>> <u>Keri</u> <u>attended</u> the conference, but <u>she</u> <u>did</u> not <u>attend</u> Bob's seminar.

Writing Workshop

Activity A. Writing Practice

Instructions: Describe the room you are in. List the tangible aspects of the room first—tangible things are those that you can see, touch, and even smell. Next, explore the intangible aspects of the room: what kinds of activities and feelings are attached to the room and why? How does the room make you feel?

Activity B. Journal

Instructions: Identify a goal that you want to achieve, such as losing weight, improving your diet, getting rid of clutter, getting organized, improving your relationships, and so on. Describe the goal in detail. What changes can you make to achieve this goal? List individual steps.

Skills Workshop

Worksheet 1: Identifying Simple Subjects and Verbs

Instructions: In each of the following sentences, first identify the verb and then its subject; underline the verb twice and the subject once. Some sentences have an implied subject, such as *you understood* or *I understood*.

If you can, work with a partner on this exercise.

Examples: The library closed at 9 p.m. on Friday.

The <u>library</u> <u>closed</u> at 9 p.m. on Friday.

Invite everyone in the department to the exhibit and reception.

(<u>You</u>) <u>Invite</u> everyone in the department to the exhibit and reception.

1. Margaret prefers to assist me on this project.

2. The order contained too many unnecessary products.

3. I thanked the new engineer for fixing the electrical problem.

4. Thank you for asking that question.

5. Our new program will begin in one month.

6. Mr. Jarris spoke about the plan in detail at our last meeting.

7. Examine the order carefully before sending it out.

8. My assistant gave me the information on Monday.

9. See the director before you leave today.

10. I am pleased that you are able to join our staff.

11. My new class in business management begins next month.

12. Your response is needed by the director immediately.

13. Will you be able to give the director your response today?

14. Please thank the participants for sharing valuable information with us.

15. Do you have an account at the First National Bank?

16. Our new bank offers great promotional items for its customers.

17. Joseph Campbell encouraged people to find their bliss in life.

18. What are you doing to improve your life's journey?

Worksheet 2: Identifying Compound Subjects and Compound Verbs

Instructions: In each of the following sentences, first identify the verb and then its subject; underline the verb twice and the subject once. Since the sentences have compound verbs and subjects, each subject and verb may consist of two or more words. Also, some sentences have an implied subject, such as *you understood* or *I understood*. If you can, work with a partner on this exercise.

Example: The library and offices close at noon but reopen at 1 p.m.

The <u>library</u> and <u>offices</u> <u>close</u> at noon but <u>reopen</u> at 1 p.m.

1. Juan and Marissa attended the meeting and participated in the discussion.

2. Identify and eliminate excess information in your paper.

3. You and your teammate should prepare the report and present it to the committee.

4. Martin and Silvia rejected the offer and suggested new negations.

5. Your sister or cousin can encourage you and provide you with support.

6. Your interests and hobbies contribute to your profile but do not count for experience.

7. You should compose a new resume and include three references.

8. You should also contact your references and ask for permission to list them on your resume.

9. Giorg and I will host the event and appreciate your attendance.

10. Bankers and brokers have exciting jobs but need to put in long hours.

Worksheet 3: Identifying Subjects and Verbs in Compound Sentences

Instructions: In each of the following sentences, identify the verb and then its subject for each main clause; underline the verb twice and the subject once. Some sentences have an implied subject, such as *you understood* or *I understood*. If you can, work with a partner on this exercise.

Example: The library closes at noon, but the offices remain open until 1 p.m.

The <u>library</u> <u>closes</u> at noon, but the <u>offices</u> <u>remain</u> open until 1 p.m.

1. Thank the participants, and let them know how to find the resources.

2. Our instructions were not clear, but our task was completed successfully.

3. Jeremy started his own landscaping business, and he is quite busy now.

4. Call him to see if he needs help, and you might have a part-time job.

5. Tell him about your previous experience, or he may not realize your qualifications.

6. Thank you for getting the project to me early, for I was in a time crunch.

7. Some resumes include too much information, so we take that into consideration.

8. Identify your interests, and find time to build them into your schedule.

9. Your skills will help you, and your attitude will ensure your success.

10. Mark your calendar for April 15, and attend this event with a friend.

End Notes

1. Karen Elizabeth Gordon, *The Deluxe Transitive Vampire*, Pantheon Books, New York, 1993, page 3.

2. Jim W. Corder and John J. Ruszkiewicz, *Handbook of Current English*, HarperCollins Publishers, 1989, page 29.

3

Conjunctions, Phrases, and Clauses

This lesson equips you with information that will make your work with commas easier and more meaningful. In fact, the pre-work in this lesson fills an important knowledge gap. The good news is that you will be able to use some of the principles in this lesson not only to make your writing correct but also to improve your writing style. So let's get started.

What Are Conjunctions?

Along with subjects and verbs, conjunctions play a critical role in grammar, punctuation, and writing style. Conjunctions are words that connect ideas and show relationships.

The other important role that conjunctions perform is that they often signal where to place a comma or a semicolon, which you will learn about in detail in the lessons that follow. The three types of conjunctions are:

- Coordinating Conjunctions

- Subordinating Conjunctions

- Adverbial Conjunctions

Along with subjects and verbs, conjunctions play a critical role in grammar, punctuation, and writing style. Learning about conjunctions will help you gain more control of your writing: you will become aware of how to use conjunctions to make transitions in your writing and assist your reader in understanding your key points.

As you use conjunctions more effectively, your writing style will improve. By pulling the reader's thinking along with yours, you help the reader draw conclusions. Conjunctions focus the reader on key points, making writing clearer and easier to understand.

Though you still might prefer to skip ahead because these terms sound complicated, realize that it will only take a bit of practice to use the terms *coordinating*, *subordinating*, and *adverbial* with ease.

Now let's get to work on conjunctions. Your goal in this lesson is to become familiar with these terms and learn a few examples in each category. Later in this lesson, you will learn more about the role conjunctions play in clauses, phrases, and sentence fragments.

What Are Coordinating Conjunctions?

Coordinating conjunctions connect equal grammatical parts. There are only seven of them, and they are as follows:

and   but   or   for   nor   so   yet

Together they spell the acronym F A N B O Y S, making it easier for you to remember them. The most commonly used coordinating conjunctions are *and, but,* and *or*.

The *equal grammatical parts* that conjunctions connect are *sentences*, *words*, and *phrases*, which you will learn more about in Lesson 4.

Before moving on, close your eyes for a moment to see how many coordinating conjunctions you can remember. After you open your eyes, jot them down in the space below. Writing them a few times will help you remember them.

_____

Now let's learn about subordinating conjunctions.

What Are Subordinating Conjunctions?

Subordinating conjunctions show relationships between ideas and, in the process, make one idea dependent on the other; they appear as single words or short phrases. Here is a list of some common subordinating conjunctions:

after	because	since	until
although	before	so that	when
as	even though	though	whereas
as soon as	if	unless	while

This list is not a complete list; for now, select a few of the subordinating conjunctions listed above, and memorize them. You can test whether a word or phrase is a subordinating conjunction by placing it at the beginning of a complete sentence. If the complete sentence no longer sounds complete, the word is probably a subordinating conjunction (SC). For example:

Complete sentence: Bob walked to the store.

SC added: *If* Bob walked to the store . . . what?

Complete sentence: The office manager arrived late.

SC added: *Since* the office manager arrived late . . . what?

Complete sentence: The sale begins tomorrow.

SC added: *Even though* the sale begins tomorrow . . . what?

Subordinating conjunctions do what their name implies: "to subordinate" means "to make less than." In the examples above, you have seen that when you place a subordinating conjunction at the beginning of a complete sentence, the sentence is no longer complete. This incomplete sentence is a **dependent clause**. Here is another set of examples:

Complete sentence: The attendant asked for my receipt.

Dependent clause: *When* the attendant asked for my receipt . . . what?

Complete sentence:	Our car is in the parking lot.
Dependent clause:	*Although* our car is in the parking lot . . . what?

Complete sentence:	Their committee meets this Friday.
Dependent clause:	*After* their committee meets this Friday . . . what?

Punctuating a dependent clause as if it is a complete sentence results in a **fragment**; a fragment is a common error, but a serious one.

Write three sentences below, and then go back and place a subordinating conjunction at the beginning of each of your sentences, as shown in the previous set of examples.

1. _____

   _____

2. _____

   _____

3. _____

   _____

Do you see how a subordinating conjunction can turn a complete sentence into a fragment? Now let's take a look at adverbial conjunctions.

What Are Adverbial Conjunctions?

Adverbial conjunctions bridge ideas, and they are known as *transition* words. Here are some examples of common adverbial conjunctions:

as a result	for example	in conclusion	in summary
consequently	hence	in general	therefore
finally	however	in other words	thus

Adverbial conjunctions help pull the reader's thinking along with the writer's intention. They can be used at the beginning of a sentence to introduce it, in the middle of a sentence to interrupt the flow of thought, or between two sentences to provide a bridge or transition, for example:

Introducing:	*Therefore*, I will not be able to attend the conference.
Interrupting:	The Jones Corporation, *however*, is not our vendor of choice.
Bridging:	George will attend the conference in my place; *as a result,* I will be able to assist you on the new project.

Here is another list of adverbial conjunctions and the kinds of transitions they make:

To compare or contrast:	however, in contrast, on the other hand, on the contrary, conversely, otherwise, nevertheless
To summarize:	in summary, in conclusion, as a result, thus, therefore, hence
To illustrate:	for example, for instance, hence, in general, thus, mostly
To add information:	in addition, additionally, furthermore, moreover, also, too
To show results:	fortunately, unfortunately, consequently, as usual, of course
To sequence or show time:	first, second, third, finally, meanwhile, in the meantime, to begin with
To conclude:	finally, in summary, in conclusion

You will notice that adverbial conjunctions appear as single words or short phrases. As a reader, these transition words help you identify key points the writer is making. As a writer, use these transition words in a conscious way to signal key points for your readers.

All three types of conjunctions—*coordinating*, *subordinating*, and *adverbial*—play a major role in writing style and punctuation. In the next two lessons, you will see how conjunctions function as signals for placing commas and semicolons. Next, let's take a look at the various types of phrases.

Workshop Activity

Instructions: Working with a partner, complete Worksheet 1: Identifying Conjunctions and Worksheet 2: Knowing Conjunctions, on pages 35-36.

What Is a Phrase?

A phrase is a group of related words that does not have a subject and predicate and cannot stand alone. Here are two important types of phrases and their definitions:

- **Infinitive phrase:** an infinitive along with its object or compliment and modifiers. An infinitive is the word *to* plus the base form of a verb, as in *to go, to walk*, and *to speak*.

- **Gerund phrase:** a gerund along with its object or compliment and modifiers. A gerund is formed by adding *ing* to the base form of a verb, as in *going, walking*, and *speaking*.

Examples of infinitive phrases:	Examples of gerund phrases:
to go to the store	going to the store
to buy what you need	buying what you need
to attend class on a daily basis	attending class on a daily basis
to inform the staff	informing the staff

In addition to gerund and infinitive phrases, you are probably familiar with prepositional phrases. Here is a brief reminder of how to identify a prepositional phrase:

- **Prepositional phrase:** a preposition along with a noun and its modifiers. Some common prepositions are *between, from, to, on, under, with, by*, and *along*.

Examples of prepositional phrases:

on the table	*behind* the desk
to the store	*by* the bookcase
after the meeting	*between* the two of us

Prepositional phrases do not have the same sort of structural impact on your writing that gerund and infinitive phrases have. For example, gerund and infinitive phrases need to be used consistently within a sentence.

If you were making a list of items that appeared as infinitive or gerund phrases, you would need to use *only* gerund phrases *or* infinitive phrases. Remaining consistent ensures that you achieve **parallel construction**, which is another way of saying that you represent your words and phrases *in the same grammatical form*. (For a practice exercise on parallel structure, go to www.commasrule.com.)

Gerund or infinitive phrases are not complete sentences because they do not contain a subject and a verb. However, when a gerund or infinitive phrase is long, it can give the illusion that it is a complete sentence. When a gerund or infinitive phrase is punctuated as if it were a complete sentence, the result is a **sentence fragment**. Let's take a look at sentence fragments.

What Is a Fragment?

A **fragment** is an incomplete statement that is punctuated as if it were a complete sentence. Most often, fragments come in the form of gerund phrases, infinitive phrases, or dependent clauses. The following are some examples of fragments broken down by type:

Gerund Phrases:	Walking slowly to the beach on a sunny day
	Following a list of directions precisely as given
Infinitive Phrases:	To walk slowly to the beach on a sunny day
	To follow a list of directions precisely as given
Dependent clauses:	*When* I walk slowly to the beach on a sunny day
	After Bob follows the list of directions that you gave him

How you correct a fragment depends on the type of fragment you are dealing with. Let's take a look at how to take a serious grammatical error and use a simple solution to correct it.

How Do You Correct a Sentence Fragment?

You have already seen that three common types of fragments are gerund phrases, infinitive phrases, and dependent clauses.

To correct fragments consisting of gerund and infinitive phrases, use the phrase as the <u>subject</u>, add a <u>verb</u>, and then finish your thought, as follows:

> <u>Walking slowly to the beach on a sunny day</u> <u>makes</u> most people feel good.

> <u>To walk slowly to the beach on a sunny day</u> <u>is</u> highly recommended.

Another way to correct gerund and infinitive fragments would be to use the fragment as the **object** of your sentence by adding a <u>subject</u> and a <u>verb</u>, as follows:

> George's favorite <u>activity</u> <u>is</u> **walking slowly to the beach on a sunny day**.

> <u>I</u> <u>prefer</u> **to walk slowly to the beach on a sunny day**.

Here is now to correct a fragment resulting from a dependent clause:

1. Use the dependent clause before a main clause to introduce the main clause,

2. Use the dependent clause after a main clause as a finishing thought, or

3. Remove the subordinating conjunction at the beginning of the clause.

In the sentences below, each dependent clause is italicized:

> *When I walk slowly to the beach on a sunny day*, my mind always wanders.

> I left work early *because I finished the list of directions precisely as given*.

When the subordinating conjunction is removed, a dependent clause can become a complete sentence; for example:

~~When~~ I walk slowly to the beach on a sunny day.

~~Because~~ I finished the list of directions precisely as given.

Workshop Activity

Instructions: Working with a partner, complete Worksheet 3: Identifying Sentences and Fragments, page 37.

Recap

In this lesson, you have learned about the various types of conjunctions as well as about sentence fragments and how to correct them.

> ➢ Here are the three types of conjunctions along with a few examples:

Coordinating conjunctions:	and, but, or, for, nor, so, yet
Subordinating conjunctions:	if, since, although, because, before, after, while
Adverbial conjunctions:	however, therefore, for example, consequently

> ➢ Conjunctions build bridges between ideas.

> ➢ Conjunctions provide cues about a writer's key points.

> ➢ A dependent clause, also known as a subordinate clause, begins with a subordinating conjunction.

> ➢ Phrases and dependent clauses that are punctuated as complete sentences are called fragments.

> ➢ To correct a fragment, start by identifying whether it consists of a dependent clause, an infinitive phrase, or a gerund phrase.

> ➢ When using gerunds or infinitives to make a list, remain consistent in the way that you use them so that your writing remains parallel.

Writing Workshop

Activity A. Writing Practice

Instructions: Use the following list of words, phrases, and clauses to build complete sentences. Identify the subject and verb of each as well as any coordinating conjunctions (CC), subordinating conjunctions (SC), or adverbial conjunctions (AC).

1. walking, swimming, and running

2. going to the store to buy

3. If I were you

4. I wish that I were able to

5. Learning to write

6. When my best friend says

7. If I could have any job in the world

8. Going to college

9. Pizza

10. The best advice anyone ever gave me

Activity B. Journal

Instructions: How are you doing with your goal? For at least two of your journal entries this week, write details about the progress you are making as well as what is holding you back. Also jot down the details: if losing weight is your goal, keep a food journal. If getting your finances in line is your goal, make a list of all of your purchases. If getting organized is your goal, list the actions you took to get things in order and what you need to do next. *Now go for it!*

Skills Workshop

Worksheet 1: Identifying Conjunctions

Instructions: In the following sentences, circle the coordinating, subordinating, and adverbial conjunctions and identify them as follows:

Coordinating conjunctions:	CC
Subordinating conjunctions:	SC
Adverbial conjunctions:	AC

Also, identify the verb of each main clause by underlining it twice and the subject by underlining it once. (The adverbial conjunction is shown in bold in the example.)

Example: Missy gave the report; however, she did not include your data.

Corrected: Missy gave the report; **however,** she did not include your data. (AC)

1. Although we were asked to join the group, we declined their invitation.

2. Marcus helped us with our plans; however, he was not in town for the celebration.

3. The new manager implemented the policy, and she asked that each of us follow it.

4. While our company does not have paid leave, it is generous with bonuses.

5. Feel free, therefore, to submit your resume online anytime before the 7th of September.

6. Consequently, we were not able to assist George with his plans.

7. I invited their department to the meeting, but they had other plans.

8. Dr. Martin requested the instructions, yet she did not follow them.

9. The group will meet in Boston; therefore, everyone will find the location convenient.

10. Please fill out the form, and return it at your convenience.

Worksheet 2: Knowing Conjunctions

Instructions: List four conjunctions for each category in the spaces provided:

Coordinating conjunctions:

_____ _____ _____ _____

Subordinating conjunctions:

_____ _____ _____ _____

Adverbial conjunctions:

_____ _____ _____ _____

Key Ideas

Instructions: Use the following fill-in-the-blanks to define the three types of conjunctions:

1. Coordinating conjunctions connect _____ grammatical parts.

2. Subordinating conjunctions show relationships between ideas and, in the process, make one idea _____ on the other.

3. Adverbial conjunctions build bridges between ideas of equal importance: they are known as _____ words.

Worksheet 3: Identifying Sentences and Fragments.

Instructions: For the following, identify whether each is a complete sentence (S) or a fragment (F). For those that are complete sentences, underline the subject once and the verb twice.

Examples: __F__ Going to the store every Saturday to buy groceries.

__S__ Buying groceries is a task that I enjoy on most days.

_____ 1. While George and I went to the store last week to buy some office supplies.

_____ 2. George suggested that we go to the new store located in the mall.

_____ 3. Since it was a holiday, getting there early to find parking nearby without walking a mile.

_____ 4. The new office supply store had everything that we needed and more.

_____ 5. Of course, adding a few items such as a stapler that weren't on my list.

_____ 6. Adding all these extra things to the shopping cart irritated George.

_____ 7. Though we are still friends, we may never go shopping together again.

_____ 8. Shopping for office supplies is something that I prefer to do alone anyway.

_____ 9. When you go shopping with someone like George who doesn't like to shop.

_____ 10. Making a list is a good idea, though.

_____ 11. When you buy things that aren't on your list, watch out so that you don't make compulsive choices.

_____ 12. Items that you don't need or won't use and that create clutter.

_____ 13. Some items look appealing at the moment but are useless in the long-run.

_____ 14. A professional shopper who knows what to buy and who doesn't end up with things just because they are good deals.

_____ 15. The next time that you go shopping, make a list and go with someone who is patient.

4

Comma Rules

Before learning how to use commas correctly, let's *clean the slate*, so to speak. In other words, to avoid using a comma for a whim or a pause, apply the following motto:

When in doubt, leave it out.

Your goal now is to use a comma *only* if you know the valid rule that applies to using it. Here is an overview of basic comma rules:

1. The sentence core rules: do not separate the <u>subject</u> and the <u>verb</u> of a sentence with only *one* comma.
2. **Conjunction**: put a comma before a coordinating conjunction, such as *and* or *but*, when it connects two independent clauses.
3. **Series**: put a comma between items in a series.
4. **Introductory**: put a comma after a word, phrase, or dependent clause that introduces an independent clause.
5. **Nonrestrictive**: use commas to set off words and phrases nonessential to the meaning of the sentence.
6. **Parenthetical Expression**: use commas to set off a word or expression that interrupts the flow of a sentence.
7. **Direct Address**: use commas to set off the name of a person addressed directly.
8. **Appositive**: use commas to set off the restatement of a noun or pronoun.
9. **Addresses and Dates**: use commas to set off the parts of addresses and dates.
10. **Words Omitted**: use a comma to indicate a word is omitted.
11. **Direct Quotation**: use commas to set off a direct quotation within a sentence.
12. **Contrasting Expression or Afterthought**: use commas to separate a contrasting expression or afterthought from the main clause.

Comma rules vary slightly from source to source. The rules presented here are consistent with other sources, but they may appear more detailed than some and less detailed than others. This approach is that it instructs you on how to use commas without going into detail about the exceptions, which can be confusing. If you find yourself writing a complicated sentence, consider simplifying your sentence by breaking down the information into more than one sentence. Simplicity is key to reader-friendly writing, which these comma rules help you achieve.

Rule 1: The Sentence Core Rules

Do not separate a subject and verb with only one comma.

Though this is somewhat of a rogue rule in that it does not indicate where you need to place a comma, this rule keeps you from making serious errors. As you already know, the sentence core is the critical point at which grammar and writing cross paths. The sentence core is the starting point of understanding grammar, and the sentence core is the most powerful element of any sentence.

As you work through these comma rules, you will find that setting off information with a pair of commas is acceptable. However, if you find yourself putting one comma between a subject and verb—take out the comma *or* see if a second comma is needed!

Now let's review the remainder of the 12 comma rules, all of which give you guidance on when you should use commas.

Rule 2: Conjunction (CONJ)

Put a comma before a coordinating conjunction, such as *and* or *but*, when it connects two independent clauses.

As you read the examples below, identify each independent clause (the subject of each clause is underlined once, and the verb twice, making the sentence core apparent at a glance):

Bill stayed late, *and* he worked on the proposal.

The book was left at the front desk, *but* George did not pick it up.

Be careful *not* to add a comma before a coordinating conjunction when only the second part of a compound verb follows it, for example:

Incorrect: <u>Bob</u> <u>worked</u> on the proposal, *and* <u>sent</u> it to my attorney.

Corrected: <u>Bob</u> <u>worked</u> on the proposal *and* <u>sent</u> it to my attorney.

However, make sure that you put a comma before coordinating conjunction when an independent clause precedes it and follows it, for example:

Incorrect: The <u>idea</u> to implement the project <u>was</u> good *so* <u>we</u> <u>plan</u> to start next week.

Corrected: The <u>idea</u> to implement the project <u>was</u> good, *so* <u>we</u> <u>plan</u> to start next week.

The sentence above marked "incorrect" is an example of a **run-on sentence**: *two or more sentences coming together without sufficient punctuation*. After working on the Skill Builder, you will learn another comma rule also based on the use of coordinating conjunctions, Rule 2: Comma Series.

Skill Builder

Rule 2: Conjunction (CONJ)

Instructions: Place commas where needed in the following sentences. For each main clause, underline the subject once and the verb twice, for example:

Incorrect: Jodie assisted with the last project so Christopher will help us with this one.

Corrected: <u>Jodie</u> <u>assisted</u> with the last project, so <u>Christopher</u> <u>will</u> <u>help</u> us with this one.

1. Mark Mallory is the new district manager and he starts on Monday.
2. Mark will be an inspiration to our staff and an excellent spokesperson for our product.
3. You can leave him a message but he will not be able to reply until next week.

4. The office in St. Louis also has a new manager and her name is Alicia Rivera.

5. Mail your information now and expect a reply within the next week.

Note: See page 69 for the answer key to the above sentences.

> **REVIEW POINT** Always remember to identify the verb first and then the subject, which precedes the verb in statements. Also do not forget that at times a sentence will have an "understood" or "implied" subject, for example:
>
> (You) Give your information to Lucile.
>
> (I) Thank you for your help.
>
> When you have difficulty identifying a subject that precedes the verb, ask yourself if the subject could be an implied subject such as *you understood* (You) or *I understood* (I).

Rule 3: Series (SER)

Put a comma between items in a series.

A series consists of at least three items, and you may have learned that the comma before the conjunction is not required. That is true. Although the comma before the conjunction *and* is not required, it is preferred, for example:

I <u>brought</u> potatoes, peas, *and* carrots to the pot luck.

The <u>estate</u> <u>was</u> <u>left</u> to Robert, Rose, Charles, *and* Sophie.

My favorite activities are walking, doing yoga, *and* swimming.

In the first example, would you prepare the "potatoes, peas, and carrots" separately or mixed? What if the comma were missing after *peas*, as in "potatoes, peas and carrots." Would you prepare them separately or mixed?

In the second example, would the estate necessarily be split the same way if the comma after Charles were missing? For example:

The estate was left to Robert, Rose, Charles *and* Sophie.

In fact, the above sentence is open for debate. Some could argue that the estate should be split only three ways, with Charles and Sophie splitting a third. For clarity, separate each entity (or separate individual) with a comma.

Another mistake that writers make is to separate *only two items* with a comma, especially when the items are long phrases (shown in italics below):

Incorrect:	The <u>assistant</u> <u>provided</u> *a series of examples*, and *a good recap of the meeting.*
Corrected:	The <u>assistant</u> <u>provided</u> *a series of examples* and *a good recap of the meeting.*

After you complete the Skill Builder, you will work on Rule 3: Comma Introductory, a rule that involves subordinating and adverbial conjunctions.

Skill Builder

Rule 3: Series (SER)

Instructions: Place commas where needed in the following sentences. For each main clause, underline the subject once and the verb twice, for example:

Incorrect:	Jerry asked for squash peas and carrots.
Corrected:	<u>Jerry</u> <u>asked</u> for squash, peas, and carrots.

1. We were assigned Conference Rooms A and B on the first floor.

2. Make sure that you bring your laptop cell phone and client list to the meeting.
3. You should arrange the meeting call your manager and submit your proposal.
4. Mitchell Helen and Sally conducted the workshop on culinary science.
5. They gave a workshop for Elaine Arlene Donald and Joanne on preparing cutting and storing vegetables.

Note: See page 69 for the answer key to the above sentences.

REVIEW POINT As a refresher, here are the three types of conjunctions that play a role in punctuation, along with a few examples of each:

Coordinating conjunctions:	and, but, or, nor, so, yet
Subordinating conjunctions:	if, after, while, when, as, as soon as, although, because
Adverbial conjunctions:	however, therefore, thus, for example, in conclusion

Conjunctions also play a role in creating a reader-friendly writing style because they cue the reader to the meaning you are conveying.

Rule 4: Introductory (INTRO)

Put a comma after a *word*, *phrase*, or *dependent clause* that introduces an independent clause.

Since this rule is a bit complicated, let's break it down into the various parts: *word*, *phrase*, and *dependent clause*.

- **Word:** in general, *word* refers to an adverbial conjunction such as *therefore*, *however*, and *consequently*, among others.

    However, I <u>was</u> not <u>able</u> to attend the conference.

    Therefore, <u>we</u> <u>will convene</u> the meeting in Boston this year.

- **Phrase:** in general, *phrase* refers to a prepositional phrase, gerund phrase, or infinitive phrase.

> *During that time*, he spoke about the plan in detail.
>
> *Leaving my bags at the airport*, I took a taxi into the city.
>
> *To arrive earlier*, Michael rearranged his entire schedule.

- **Dependent clause:** a dependent clause begins with a subordinating conjunction, such as *since, because, although, while, if,* and so on.

> *Although* my <u>calendar</u> <u>is</u> full, <u>we</u> <u>can meet</u> this Friday morning.
>
> *Before* <u>you</u> <u>arrive</u> at my office, <u>(you)</u> <u>call</u> my assistant.
>
> *Until* <u>I</u> <u>am</u> available, <u>you</u> <u>can use</u> an extra office to work.

A common mistake is to place a comma after a subordinating conjunction, for example:

Incorrect: *Although*, the information is timely, we cannot use it.

Corrected: *Although* the information is timely, we cannot use it.

Place the comma after the dependent clause, *not* after the subordinating conjunction! After you complete the Skill Builder, you will learn that some commas come in sets, as with Rule 4: Comma Nonrestrictive.

Skill Builder

Rule 4: Introductory (INTRO)

Instructions: Place commas where needed in the following sentences. For each main clause, underline the subject once and the verb twice:

Incorrect: Although Mary flew to Boston she arrived a day late.

Corrected: Although <u>Mary</u> <u>flew</u> to Boston, <u>she</u> <u>arrived</u> late.

1. Because the letter arrived late we were not able to respond on time.
2. However we were given an extension.

3. Although the extra time helped us we still felt pressured for time.

4. To get another extension George called their office.

5. Fortunately the office manager was agreeable to our request.

Note: See page 69 for the answer key to the sentences above.

REVIEW POINT The subject and verb form the sentence core, the powerhouse of your sentence. Separating the subject and verb with *only one comma* creates a major grammatical error. (See Rule 12, pages 39-40.)

Do not *separate a subject and verb with just one comma.*

You will learn, however, that you can separate a subject and verb with a *set* of commas.

Rule 5: Nonrestrictive (NR)

Use commas to set off explanations that are nonessential to the meaning of the sentence.

The key to understanding this rule lies in the difference between the meaning of the words *restrictive* and *nonrestrictive*.

- **Restrictive information** is *essential* and should not be set off with commas.

- **Nonrestrictive information** is *not essential* and can be set off with commas.

Whenever you set off information between two commas, you are implying that the information can be removed without disturbing the structure or meaning of the sentence.

Nonrestrictive elements often come in the form of "who" or "which" clauses. Read the following two examples that illustrate this rule (*who* clauses are shown in italics):

Alice Walker, *who is a prestigious author*, will be the keynote speaker.

The woman *who is a prestigious author* will be the keynote speaker.

In the first example above, you would still know who the keynote speaker would be even if the *who* clause were removed:

Alice Walker will be the keynote speaker.

However, in the second example, the meaning of the sentence would be unclear if the *who* clause were removed:

The woman will be the keynote speaker. *Which woman?*

In fact, all commas that come in sets imply that the information set off by the commas can be removed; so here is another reminder of how to use commas with *essential* and *nonessential* elements:

- Essential information is restrictive and should not be set off with commas.

- Nonessential information is nonrestrictive and can be set off with commas.

Complete the following Skill Builder to test your understanding.

Skill Builder

Rule 5: Nonrestrictive (NR)

Instructions: Place commas where needed in the following sentences. For each main clause, underline the subject once and the verb twice. The essential and nonessential clauses are shown in italics, for example:

Incorrect:	The artist *who designed our brochure* lives in New Orleans.
Corrected:	The <u>artist</u> *who designed our brochure* <u>lives</u> in New Orleans. (no commas needed)

1. Our manager *who specializes in project grants* will assist you with this issue.

2. Tomas Phillips *who works only on weekends* will call you soon.

3. The paralegal *who researched this lawsuit* is not available.

4. Nick Richards *who is in a meeting until 3 p.m.* can answer your question.

5. Your new contract *which we mailed yesterday* should arrive by Friday.

Note: See page 70 for the answer key to the above sentences.

Rule 6: Parenthetical (PAR)

Use commas to set off a word or expression that interrupts the flow of a sentence.

This rule applies to adverbial conjunctions or other short phrases interjected into a sentence. By interrupting the flow of the sentence, a parenthetical expression places stress on the words immediately preceding it or following it. These elements should be set off with commas because they are nonessential and can be removed.

The following three examples show parenthetical expressions (shown in italics) set off with commas. Can you see how each could be removed, leaving the sentence complete and clear in meaning?

Mr. Connors, *however*, arrived after the opening ceremony.

You can, *therefore*, place your order after 5 p.m. today.

The project, *in my opinion*, needs improvement.

A common mistake occurs when a writer uses a semicolon in place of one of the commas, for example:

Incorrect: Ms. Philippe; in fact, approved the request last week.

Corrected: Ms. Philippe, in fact, approved the request last week.

Though a semicolon *can* precede an adverbial conjunction, that construction involves two sentences. In those cases, the adverbial conjunction functions as a bridge or a transition rather than an interrupter. (See Lesson 5: Semicolons)

Another common mistake occurs when a writer uses only one comma rather than a set of commas, for example:

Incorrect: Our sales representative, therefore will assist you at your convenience.

Corrected: Our sales representative, therefore, will assist you at your convenience.

Incorrect: Mr. Jones, however will plan this year's event.

Corrected: Mr. Jones, however, will plan this year's event.

Even though adverbial conjunctions are usually nonessential elements in terms of sentence structure, they play an important role in writing style. Adverbial conjunctions give vital clues to meaning, helping your reader identify key points. After working on the Skill Builder below, you will learn Rule 6: Direct Address.

Skill Builder

Rule 6: Parenthetical (PAR)

Instructions: Place commas where needed in the following sentences. For each main clause, underline the subject once and the verb twice:

Incorrect: Our contract however did not include charges for delivery.

Corrected: Our <u>contract</u>, however, <u><u>did</u></u> not <u><u>include</u></u> charges for delivery.

1. Customer service I believe can best assist you with this issue.
2. T. J. therefore will work this weekend in my place.
3. Our invoice unfortunately was submitted incorrectly.
4. The new contract in my opinion meets specifications.
5. Brown Company of course recommended us to a vendor.

Note: See page 70 for the answer key to the above sentences.

WRITING TIP *A Note about Style*: Comma Parenthetical Expression (PE) shows you the correct way to punctuate a sentence when an adverbial conjunction occurs in the middle of a sentence. However, you can often make your sentence more reader friendly by moving the adverbial conjunction to the beginning of the sentence, for example:

> *Therefore*, our sales representative will assist you.
>
> *In fact*, Mr. Philippe approved the request.
>
> *In my opinion*, the project needs improvement.

In fact, writers often interject a comment such as "I believe" or "I think" at the beginning of a sentence. These types of expressions can generally be removed, improving the flow of the sentence and making the meaning clearer. Use parenthetical expressions only when they make your meaning clearer.

Rule 7: Direct Address (DA)

Use commas to set off the name or title of a person addressed directly.

Often the name of the person being addressed directly appears at the beginning of the sentence, but the name can also appear in the middle of the sentence or at the end of it, as shown below:

> *Donald*, <u>you</u> <u>can</u> <u>arrange</u> the meeting in Dallas or Fort Worth.
>
> <u>I</u> <u>gave</u> the invitation to everyone in the department, *Marge*.
>
> Your <u>instructions</u>, *Professor*, <u>were</u> clear and to the point.

In each of the above examples, notice that the name of the person being addressed is *not* the subject of the sentence. The following sentences also contain a direct address, but the subject of each sentence is implied. As you read the sentences, ask yourself *who* is performing the action of the verb:

> <u>Thank</u> you, *Astrid*, for speaking on my behalf.
>
> <u>Feel</u> free to call my office at your convenience, *David*.
>
> *Traci*, please <u>assist</u> me with the spring conference.

In the first sentence above, the implied subject is *I understood*; in the second and third, the implied subject is *you understood*:

> *I* <u>thank</u> you, Astrid, for speaking on my behalf.
>
> *You* <u>feel</u> free to call my office at your convenience, David.
>
> Traci, *<u>you</u>* please <u>assist</u> me with the spring conference.

You will find that in sentences that contain a direct address, the subject is often implied.

Complete the Skill Builder below before moving on to Comma Rule 7: Comma Appositive.

Skill Builder

Rule 7: Direct Address (DA)

Instructions: Place commas where needed in the following sentences. For each main clause, underline the subject once and the verb twice:

Incorrect: Johnny you should study that problem in more depth.

Corrected: Johnny, <u>you</u> <u>should</u> <u>study</u> that problem in more depth.

1. Give your report to the auditor by Friday Marcel.
2. Jason do you have tickets for the game?
3. Doctor I would like to know the results of my tests.
4. Would you like to attend the banquet Alice?
5. Thank you for inviting me George.

Note: See page 70 for the answer key to the sentences above.

Rule 8: Appositive (AP)

Use commas to set off the restatement of a noun or pronoun.

With an appositive, an equivalency exists between the noun and its descriptor. In the examples below, the appositives are show in italics:

<u>Carolyn</u>, *my co-worker from Atlanta*, <u>requested</u> the date.

<u>Mr. Johns</u>, *the building commissioner*, <u>refused</u> to give us a permit.

To check to see if the descriptor is an appositive, ask yourself questions such as the following:

Who is Carolyn?   My co-worker from Atlanta.

Who is my co-worker from Atlanta? Carolyn.

Who is Mr. Johns? The building commissioner.

Who is the building commissioner? Mr. Johns.

For an appositive that occurs in the middle of a sentence, using only one comma not only creates a mistake but also changes the meaning of the sentence. Notice how the following sentences differ in meaning:

Incorrect: Josef, my former <u>boss</u> <u>gave</u> me the information.

Corrected: Josef, my former boss, <u>gave</u> me the information.

In the first sentence above, the subject shifts to "boss" because of Rule 12 which states, "Do not separate a subject and verb with only one comma." In other words, leaving out the comma after "Josef" changes the meaning of the sentence because grammar dictates that the real subject becomes "boss."

Appositives are not always nonrestrictive; an appositive can be restrictive, which means that it is essential for clear meaning. For example, let's say that you have five brothers and one of them is named Charles, who is joining you for dinner.

Appositive: My brother, Charles, will join us for dinner.

If you took "Charles" out of the above sentence, would the reader know which brother would join you for dinner? Because of the commas, the above sentence translates to: *My brother will join us for dinner.* Thus, for a restricted appositive, omit the commas, as follows:

Restricted Appositive: My brother Charles will join us for dinner.

A **restricted appositive**, as illustrated by the sentence above, should not be set off with commas. However, for now focus on identifying nonrestrictive appositives, which are far more common and are set off with commas.

Complete the Skill Builder below before going on to Rule 8: Addresses and Dates.

Skill Builder

Rule 8: Appositive (AP)

Instructions: Place commas where needed in the following sentences. For extra practice, underline the subject once and the verb twice in each main clause, for example:

Incorrect: Elaine my cousin taught business education subjects.

Corrected: Elaine, my cousin, taught business education subjects.

1. Jacob Seinfeld our associate director decided to hire Williams.

2. My best friend Janet Sparacio applied for a job here.

3. Jim Martinez the registrar approved your request.

4. The department chair Dr. George Schmidt did not receive your transcript.

5. The director asked Clair my sister to join us for dinner.

Note: See page 70 for the answer key to the above sentences.

Rule 9: Addresses and Dates (AD)

Use commas to set off the parts of addresses and dates.

The term "set off" means that you put commas on both sides of the part of the address or date to show separation. For example, notice how the commas surround "Massachusetts" and "California" as well as "August 15":

Boston, Massachusetts, is the best city to host the conference.

Sally has worked in Long Beach, California, for the past five years.

On Wednesday, August 15, my friends celebrated the Ferragosta.

Does it surprise you to learn that a comma is required *after* the state name when a city and state are written together? If so, you are not alone; the following mistake is common:

Incorrect: Dallas, <u>Texas</u> <u>is</u> a great city to start a new business.

Corrected: <u>Dallas</u>, Texas, <u>is</u> a great city to start a new business.

The same is true for dates, with the second comma in the set being incorrectly left off, as follows:

Incorrect: Jerome listed August 15, 2005 as his start date.

Corrected: Jerome listed August 15, 2005, as his start date.

Another type of error occurs when a writer puts a comma between the month and the day, for example:

Incorrect: September, 10, 2006 was the date on the application.

Corrected: September 10, 2006, was the date on the application.

Putting a comma between the month and the day (September, 10) *never* occurs! After you complete the Skill Builder for this rule, you will work on comma Rule 9: Words Omitted.

Skill Builder

Rule 9: Addresses and Dates (AD)

Instructions: Place commas where needed in the following sentences. For extra practice, underline the subject once and the verb twice in each main clause, for example:

Incorrect: The conference is planned for August 19 2009 in Denver Colorado.

Corrected: The <u>conference</u> <u>is</u> <u>planned</u> for August 19, 2009, in Denver, Colorado.

1. Send your application by Friday December 15 to my assistant.
2. San Antonio Texas has a River Walk and Conference Center.
3. Would you prefer to meet in Myrtle Minnesota or Des Moines Iowa?

4. Springfield Massachusetts continues to be my selection.

5. We arrived in Chicago Illinois on May 22 2008 to prepare for the event.

Note: See page 71 for the answer key to the above sentences.

Rule 10: Word Omitted (WO)

Use a comma in place of a word that has been omitted when its omission affects the flow of the sentence.

This type of comma occurs less frequently than most of the others; most of the time, the word that has been omitted is either *that* or *and*.

The problem is *that* the current situation is quite grim.

The problem is, the current situation is quite grim.

Mr. Adams presented the long *and* boring report to the board.

Mr. Adams presented the long, boring report to the board.

Work on the Skill Builder before moving on to Rule 10: Comma Quotation.

Skill Builder

Rule 10: Word Omitted (WO)

Instructions: Place commas where needed in the following sentences. Underline the subject once and the verb twice for each main clause:

Incorrect: My suggestion is you should contain the situation now.

Corrected: My suggestion is, you should contain the situation now. (WO)

Corrected: My suggestion is that you should contain the situation now.

1. The president shared two intriguing confidential reports.

2. The photo shoot is on Tuesday at 5 p.m. on Wednesday at 6 p.m.

3. The problem is some of the results are not yet known.

4. Leave the materials with Alicia at the Westin with Marcia at the Hilton.

5. Silvana presented a short exciting PowerPoint on Italy.

Note: See page 71 for the answer key to the above sentences.

Rule 11: Direct Quotation (DQ)

Use commas to set off a direct quotation within a sentence.

A direct quotation is a person's exact words. In comparison, an indirect quotation does not give a speaker's exact words and would *not* be set off with commas.

Direct Quotation:	Gabrielle said, "I have a 9 o'clock appointment," and then left abruptly.
Indirect Quotation:	Gabrielle said that she had a 9 o'clock appointment and then left abruptly.
Direct Quotation:	Dr. Gorman asked, "Is the environment experiencing global warming at a faster rate than previously predicted?"
Indirect Quotation:	Dr. Gorman asked whether the environment is experiencing global warming at a faster rate than previously predicted.

An exception to this rule relates to short quotations: a short quotation built into the flow of a sentence does not need to be set off with commas.

Short Quotations:	Marian shouted "Help!" as she slid on the ice.
	My boss told me "Do not sweat the small stuff" before he let me go.
	The advice "Give the project your best this time" sounded patronizing rather than encouraging.

In each of the direct quotations, whether set off with commas or blending with the flow of the sentence, the first word of the quotation is capitalized.

A note about quotation and punctuation placement:
- Commas and periods always go on the inside of quotation marks.
- Semicolons and colons always go on the outside of quotation marks.
- Exclamation marks and question marks are placed based on meaning and can go on the inside or outside of quotation marks.
- Never double punctuate at the end of a sentence.

You will learn about each of the above points in detail when you work on Lesson 8: Quotation Marks, Apostrophes, and Hyphens. Do the following Skill Builder before moving to your last substantial comma rule, Rule 11: Comma Contrasting Expression or Afterthought.

Skill Builder

Rule 11: Direct Quotation (DQ)

Instructions: Place commas where needed in the following sentences. Underline the subject once and the verb twice for each main clause.

Incorrect:	Jeffery insisted go back to the beginning before you decide to give up!
Corrected:	Jeffery insisted, "Go back to the beginning before you decide to give up!"

1. Patrick shouted get back! before we had a chance to see the falling debris.

2. According to Tyler all children can learn if they find an interest in what is taught.

3. My father warned me when you choose an insurance company, find one with good customer service.

4. Sharon encouraged me by yelling go for the gold as I was starting the race.

5. Lenny told me good luck on your exam before I left this morning.

Note: See page 71 for the answer key to the above sentences.

Rule 12: Contrasting Expression or Afterthought (CEA)

Use a comma to separate a contrasting expression or afterthought from the main clause.

A contrasting expression or afterthought adds an interesting twist to writing style. The expression at the end of the sentence certainly gets the reader's attention, for example:

> Go ahead and put the property on the market, if you can.

> I asked for the information so that I could process the sale, not to lose it.

> My cousin Buddy, not my brother Chuck, drove me to the airport.

In fact, omitting the CEA comma is not a serious error; however, using the CEA comma makes your comments stand out and gives your writing a more conversational flow.

After you complete the Skill Builder below, complete the worksheets at the end of this lesson so that you get the practice that you need.

Skill Builder

Rule 12: Contrasting Expression or Afterthought (CEA)

Instructions: Place commas where needed in the following sentences. For extra practice, underline the subject once and the verb twice in each main clause, for example:

Incorrect: Elaine attended Southern State University not Northern State.

Corrected: Elaine attended Southern State University, not Northern State.

1. You will find the manuscript in John's office not in Bob's.

2. Marcus secured the contract but only after negotiating for hours.

3. Chair the budget committee if you prefer.

4. Lester rather than Dan received the award.

5. Work to achieve your dreams not to run away from your fears.

Note: See page 72 for the answer key to the above sentences.

Workshop Activity

Instructions: Work with a partner to complete the Skills Workshop. After you complete Worksheets 1, 2, 3, and 4, you will be ready to move on to Lesson 5: Semicolon Rules.

Recap

Knowing the basic comma rules will make a difference in the quality of your writing and your confidence. Commit yourself to completing the practice worksheets at the end of this lesson, following the directions exactly as prescribed.

As you complete each worksheet, the instructions direct you to place commas where needed as well as to identify the reason for each comma you use. Analyzing comma use in this way may seem challenging at first; however, this approach ensures that you will not only be correct but also be able to explain why.

The more you practice, the easier this task will become. And the good news is that you will learn commas in a way so that you will use them correctly and confidently for the rest of your writing career. *Now go for it!*

A summary of the comma rules that you have learned in this lesson appear on the following page.

Comma Rules

Rule 1: The Sentence Core Rules
Do not separate a subject and verb with only one comma.

Rule 2: Conjunction (CONJ)
Put a comma before a coordinating conjunction, such as *and* or *but*, when it connects two independent clauses.

Rule 3: Series (SER)
Put a comma between items in a series.

Rule 4: Introductory (INTRO)
Put a comma after a *word*, *phrase*, or *dependent clause* that introduces an independent clause.

Rule 5: Nonrestrictive (NR)
Use commas to set off nonessential words and phrases.

Rule 6: Parenthetical (PAR)
Use commas to set off a word or expression that interrupts the flow of a sentence.

Rule 7: Direct Address (DA)
Use commas to set off the name or title of a person addressed directly.

Rule 8: Appositive (AP)
Use commas to set off the restatement of a noun or pronoun.

Rule 9: Addresses and Dates (AD)
Use commas to set off the parts of addresses and dates.

Rule 10: Word Omitted (WO)
Use a comma to indicate a word is omitted when it affects the flow of the sentence.

Rule 11: Direct Quotation (DQ)
Use commas to set off direct quotations within a sentence.

Rule 12: Contrasting Expression or Afterthought (CEA)
Use a comma to separate a contrasting expression or afterthought.

Writing Workshop

Activity A. Writing Practice

Instructions: John Dewey once said, "We become what we learn." Do you agree? How can you tell when you have learned something? How does it feel when you fail . . . or succeed? When you are motivated, do you work harder to learn?

Write a short paper entitled, "What Is Learning?" If you can, discuss the above questions with a peer before you start writing.

Activity B. Journal

Instructions: Identify three people to whom you have a message to convey. Write each of them a letter. You do not need to send them the letters, but you can if you wish. In fact, you may choose to write to someone who is no longer in your life. Finally, write a letter to yourself: give yourself a pat on the back for working so hard to achieve your goals. Also give yourself a few words of encouragement for the journey ahead. Remember, you can realize your dreams as long as you keep your heart and mind focused on achieving them.

Skills Workshop

As you complete the worksheets on the following pages, indicate the reason for each comma that you use. This additional step of analysis ensures that you will make conscious, educated decisions, bringing your skills to a higher level of expertise.

Analyzing comma use in this way may seem challenging in the beginning. However, this approach ensures that you will learn commas once and for all, a benefit throughout your writing career.

Note: You will find the keys to these exercises in the **Keys to Assessments and Worksheets** located at the back of this book.

Worksheet 1: Practice for the following comma rules:

- **Conjunction (CONJ)**
- **Series (SER)**
- **Direct Address (DA)**

Instructions: Place commas where needed in the following sentences. For each main clause, underline the subject once and the verb twice. Also, indicate the name of the comma rule for each comma that you use, for example:

Incorrect: You assisted me with the project and I appreciated it.

Correct: You assisted me with the project, and I appreciated it. (CONJ)

1. I completed my report and Alice sent it to Wanda.

2. Wanda received the report but she did not yet file it with the department.

3. Thank you for letting me know about your concern Marsha.

4. Wanda will appreciate your telling her about the missing information for John Wilson Bill Jones and Mark Kramer.

5. Give Wanda the information today and you will save her some time.

6. The report often needs to be adjusted and Wanda kindly helps us with it.

7. Marsha you are wonderful to assist us with the extra work in our department.

8. You should first work on the monthly report schedules and inventory.

9. You can ask for additional time but you may not receive it.

10. The training room needs new chairs tables and flip charts.

11. Go to the mail room to get the catalog for ordering supplies Mallory.

12. The accounting department issues guidelines for expenses and someone in that department can assist you with your expense account.

13. Client lunches are included but you cannot get reimbursed for meals with friends family and co-workers.

14. File your expense account by the 15th of each month and you will receive your check by the 30th of the month.

15. Jorge thank you for following the policy as it is written.

Instructions: Now that you have had some practice, write two sentences demonstrating each of these rules:

- **Conjunction (CONJ)**

_____

_____

- **Series (SER)**

_____

_____

- **Direct Address (DA)**

_____

_____

Worksheet 2: Practice for the following comma rules:

- **Introductory (INTRO)**
- **Appositive (AP)**
- **Direct Address (DA)**

Instructions: Place commas where needed in the following sentences. For each main clause, underline the subject once and the verb twice. Also, indicate the name of the comma rule for each comma that you use, for example:

Incorrect: If you are able to assist me I would be relieved.

Correct: If you are able to assist me, I would be relieved. (INTRO)

1. While I waited for a bus I was able to complete the report.

2. However the report may need some major revisions.

3. Give me your honest opinion Mike.

4. Mr. Sisco our new office manager will use the report to make important decisions.

5. If I had known how important the report would be I would not have agreed to do it.

6. However I felt pressured to agree to do it because everyone has too much work.

7. You can ask Susan our sales representative for a second opinion.

8. When I started this job I had no idea about the long work hours.

9. However I would have taken it anyway because of its wonderful opportunities.

10. After you work here for a while you will appreciate your fellow workers.

11. Mitchell could you help Helen with the new project?

12. If you cannot help Helen at this time you should not worry about it.

13. However check back with her periodically to see how the project is going.

14. Our new vice president Melissa Lorenz scheduled a meeting for this Friday afternoon.

15. Jamie check with Melissa to find out if the entire department needs to attend.

Instructions: Now that you have had some practice, write two sentences demonstrating each of these rules:

- **Introductory (INTRO)**

_____

_____

- **Appositive (AP)**

_____

_____

- **Direct Address (DA)**

_____

_____

Worksheet 3: Practice for the following comma rules:

- **Conjunction (CONJ)**
- **Addresses and Dates (AD)**
- **Nonrestrictive (NR)**
- **Parenthetical (PAR)**

Instructions: Place commas where needed in the following sentences. For each main clause, underline the subject once and the verb twice. Also, indicate the name of the comma rule for each comma that you use, for example:

Incorrect: You are wonderful to help me and I will return the favor.

Correct: You are wonderful to help me, and I will return the favor. (CONJ)

1. Mr. Gates started a computer company and Miller decided to invest in it.

2. Miller however did not realize the potential at that time.

3. The company which is quite successful has satellites around the world.

4. He revealed that March 27 2008 will be the official kick-off date.

5. Arrive on time to the interview and you will get off to a good start.

6. We have as a result chosen another vendor.

7. The time management seminar was excellent and its cost was reasonable.

8. Your paper unfortunately did not meet the standards.

9. Our management team assessed the damages and they recommended changes.

10. On September 5 2008 we will arrive in Denver Colorado for a meeting.

11. Leadership is a vital topic but no one seems to be addressing it.

12. Simone will however assist you with the project.

Worksheet 4: Practice for the following comma rules:

- **Introductory (INTRO)**
- **Series (SER)**
- **Words Omitted (WO)**
- **Contrasting Expression or Afterthought (CEA)**

Instructions: Place commas where needed in the following sentences. For each main clause, underline the subject once and the verb twice. Also, indicate the name of the comma rule for each comma that you use, for example:

Incorrect: You are invited to the kick-off event and can bring a friend if you wish.

Correct: You are invited to the kick-off event and can bring a friend, if you wish. (CEA)

1. If you choose to attend the event let us know by the end of the day.

2. Bring a guest to the luncheon if you prefer.

3. If you need extra tickets ask Elizabeth.

4. After the awards they will serve a meal of fish potatoes and broccoli.

5. Resume the program at the north branch not at the south branch.

6. Although the offer still stands our deadline quickly approaches.

7. Before they rescind their offer give them an answer.

8. After you review the contract let us know what you think.

9. The contract can be changed but only on our terms.

10. Your feedback should include items to add delete or change.

11. The fact is your input will assist us in many ways.

12. Begin the year with a detailed comprehensive plan.

Keys to Lesson 4 Skill Builders

Key to Rule 1: Conjunction (CONJ)

1. <u>Mark Mallory</u> <u>is</u> the new district manager, and <u>he</u> <u>starts</u> on Monday. CONJ

2. <u>Mark</u> <u>will be</u> an inspiration to our staff and an excellent spokesperson for our product. (no commas)

3. <u>You</u> <u>can leave</u> him a message, but <u>he</u> <u>will</u> not <u>be</u> able to reply until next week. CONJ

4. The <u>office</u> in St. Louis also <u>has</u> a new manager, and her <u>name</u> <u>is</u> Alicia Rivera. CONJ

5. <u>You</u> <u>can mail</u> your information now and <u>expect</u> a reply within the next two weeks. (no commas)

Key to Rule 2: Series (SER)

1. <u>We</u> <u>were</u> <u>assigned</u> Conference Rooms A and B on the first floor. (no commas)

2. (<u>You</u>) <u>Make</u> sure that you bring your laptop, cell phone, and client list to the meeting. SER

3. <u>You</u> <u>should</u> <u>arrange</u> the meeting, call your manager, and submit your proposal. SER

4. <u>Mitchell</u>, <u>Helen</u>, and <u>Sally</u> <u>conducted</u> the workshop on culinary science. SER

5. <u>They</u> <u>gave</u> a workshop for Elaine, Arlene, Donald, and Joanne on preparing, cutting, and storing vegetables. SER

Key to Rule 3: Introductory (INTRO)

1. Because the <u>letter</u> <u>arrived</u> late, <u>we</u> <u>were</u> not able to respond on time. INTRO

2. However, <u>we</u> <u>were</u> <u>given</u> an extension. INTRO

3. Although the extra <u>time</u> <u>helped</u> us, <u>we</u> still <u>felt</u> pressured for time. INTRO

4. To get another extension, <u>George</u> <u>called</u> their office. INTRO

5. Fortunately, the office <u>manager</u> <u>was</u> agreeable to our request. INTRO

Key to Rule 4: Nonrestrictive (NR)

1. Our <u>manager</u> *who specializes in project grants* <u>will</u> <u>assist</u> you with this issue. (restrictive: no commas)

2. <u>Tomas Phillips</u>, *who works only on weekends,* <u>will</u> <u>call</u> you soon. NR

3. The <u>paralegal</u> *who researched this lawsuit* <u>is</u> not available. (restrictive: no commas)

4. <u>Nick Richards,</u> *who is in a meeting until 3 p.m.,* <u>can</u> <u>answer</u> your question. NR

5. Your new <u>contract</u>, *which we mailed yesterday,* <u>should</u> <u>arrive</u> by Friday. NR

Key to Rule 5: Parenthetical (PAR)

1. <u>Customer service</u>, I believe, <u>can</u> best <u>assist</u> you with this issue. PAR

2. <u>T. J.</u>, therefore, <u>will</u> <u>work</u> this weekend in my place. PAR

3. Our <u>invoice</u>, too, <u>was</u> <u>submitted</u> incorrectly. PAR

4. The new <u>contract</u>, in my opinion, <u>meets</u> specifications. PAR

5. <u>Brown Company</u>, of course, <u>recommended</u> us to a vendor. PAR

Key to Rule 6: Direct Address (DA)

1. (<u>You</u>) <u>Give</u> your report to the auditor by Friday, Marcel. DA

2. Jason, <u>do</u> <u>you</u> <u>have</u> tickets for the game? DA

3. Doctor, <u>I</u> <u>would</u> <u>like</u> to know the results of my tests. DA

4. <u>Would</u> <u>you</u> <u>like</u> to attend the banquet, Alice? DA

5. (I) <u>Thank</u> you for inviting me, George. DA

Key to Rule 7: Appositive (AP)

1. <u>Jacob Seinfeld</u>, our associate director, <u>decided</u> to hire Williams. AP

2. My best <u>friend</u>, Janet Sparacio, <u>applied</u> for a job here. AP (or no commas)

3. <u>Jim Martinez</u>, the registrar, <u>approved</u> your request. AP

4. The <u>department chair</u>, Dr. George Schmidt, <u>did</u> not <u>receive</u> your transcript. AP

5. The <u>director</u> <u>asked</u> Claire, my sister, to join us for dinner. AP

Key to Rule 8: Addresses and Dates (AD)

1. (<u>You</u>) <u>Send</u> your application by Friday, December 15, to my assistant. AD

2. <u>San Antonio</u>, Texas, <u>has</u> a River Walk and Conference Center. AD

3. <u>Would</u> <u>you</u> <u>prefer</u> to meet in Myrtle, Minnesota, or Des Moines, Iowa? AD

4. <u>Springfield</u>, Massachusetts, <u>continues</u> to be my selection. AD

5. <u>We</u> <u>arrived</u> in Chicago, Illinois, on March 15, 2008, to prepare for the event. AD

Key to Rule 9: Word Omitted (WO)

1. The <u>president</u> <u>shared</u> two intriguing, confidential reports. WO

2. The <u>crew</u> <u>scheduled</u> filming on Tuesday at 5 p.m., on Wednesday at 6 p.m. WO

3. The <u>problem</u> <u>is</u>, some of the results are not yet known. WO

4. (<u>You</u>) <u>Leave</u> the materials with Alicia at the Westin, with Marcia at the Hilton. WO

5. <u>Silvana</u> <u>presented</u> a short, exciting PowerPoint on Italy. WO

Key to Rule 10: Direct Quotation (DQ)

1. Patrick shouted "Get back!" before we had a chance to see the falling debris. DQ

2. According to Tyler, "All children can learn if they find an interest in what is taught." DQ

3. My father warned me, "When you choose an insurance company, find one with good customer service." DQ

4. Sharon encouraged me by yelling "Go for the gold!" as I was starting the race. DQ

5. Lenny told me, "Good luck on your exam," before I left this morning. DQ (or no commas)

Key to Rule 11: Contrasting Expression or Afterthought (CEA)

1. You <u>will find</u> the manuscript in John's office, not in Bob's. CEA

2. <u>Marcus</u> <u>secured</u> the contract, but only after negotiating for hours. CEA

3. <u>(You)</u> <u>Chair</u> the budget committee, if you prefer. CEA

4. <u>Lester</u>, rather than Dan, <u>received</u> the award. CEA

5. <u>(You)</u> <u>Work</u> to achieve your dreams, not to run away from your fears. CEA

5

Semicolon Rules

Most people find commas a necessity, sprinkling them throughout their writing even when unsure about how to use them correctly. It does not work that way with semicolons, however. Some people—maybe most people—develop an aversion to using semicolons, hoping to avoid them for life!

The truth is, you *can* avoid using semicolons. But if you do not use them, you are sometimes likely to put a comma where a semicolon belongs, creating a serious grammatical error. While semicolons are not similar to commas, they are similar to periods: semicolons, like periods, create major breaks in structure; for example:

- A semicolon is a full stop that is not terminal.
- A period is a full stop that is terminal.

A period brings the sentence to an end, but a semicolon does not. Most of the time, the following rule of thumb for using semicolons will work for you:

Use a semicolon in place of a period.

In other words, if you cannot use a period, you probably should not use a semicolon either.

So if you never need to use a semicolon, why use one? Though you may not yet realize it, punctuation speaks to your reader in subtle, yet powerful, ways. Here are two things to consider about the semicolon:

1. The semicolon whispers to your reader that two sentences share a key idea.

2. The semicolon alerts readers to slight shades of meaning, helping readers see connections and draw relationships.

In addition, once you use your first semicolon correctly, you are likely to feel so excited about it, you will want to use the semicolon more often just for the thrill of it! OK, so *thrill* might be a bit of a stretch; however, the more serious you become about writing, the more you will enjoy using the less common punctuation marks, such as semicolons, dashes, and ellipses (which you will learn how to use in Lesson 6). These marks give you choices and options; but more importantly, they give your voice a fingerprint and add momentum to your message.

Here are three basic semicolon rules:

1. **Semicolon No Conjunction**: use a semicolon to separate two independent clauses that are joined without a conjunction.

2. **Semicolon Bridge**: use a semicolon before and a comma after an adverbial conjunction that acts as a bridge between two independent clauses.

3. **Semicolon Because of Comma**: when a clause needs major and minor separations, use semicolons for major breaks and commas for minor breaks.

Before working on each of the semicolon rules, try to write two sentences in which you would use a semicolon correctly.

1. _____

    _____

2. _____

    _____

REVIEW POINT While you are familiar with the role conjunctions play with comma use, you are not yet familiar with the role they play with semicolon use.

- **Coordinating conjunctions** connect equal grammatical parts: and, but, or, for, nor, so, yet

- **Subordinating conjunctions** introduce dependent clauses and phrases: after, while, because, although, before, though, if, as, as soon as, and so on.

- **Adverbial conjunctions** introduce or interrupt independent clauses: however, therefore, for example, consequently, as a result, though, thus, fortunately, and so on.

Be cautious when a conjunction appears in the middle of a sentence as it may signal the use of a semicolon (see Rule 2: Semicolon Bridge and Rule 3: Semicolon Because of Commas).

Rule 1: Semicolon No Conjunction (NC)

Use a semicolon to separate two independent clauses that are joined without a conjunction.

This semicolon rule closely relates to the comma conjunction (CONJ) rule, which states "place a comma after a coordinating conjunction when it connects two independent clauses." When a conjunction is not present, the two independent clauses need to be separated by a period or a semicolon, for example:

Comma Conjunction:	Al <u>went</u> to the store, *but* he <u>forgot</u> to buy bread. (CONJ)
Semicolon No Conjunction:	Al <u>went</u> to the store; he <u>forgot</u> to buy bread. (NC)
Period:	Al <u>went</u> to the store. He <u>forgot</u> to buy bread.

Notice how each sentence has a slightly different effect based on how it is punctuated. Do you see how choppy the writing sounds in the example above which uses a period, thereby breaking up the sentences?

In general, you want to avoid short, choppy sentences, and one way to do this is to use a semicolon instead of a period. The semicolon no conjunction (NC) rule is best applied when two sentences are closely related, especially when one or both sentences are short.

The examples and practice exercises in this book are designed to help you gain a better understanding of structure. Understanding structure provides a foundation that will help you improve your editing skills as well as your writing style. Before moving to the next semicolon rule, do the practice exercises below so that you gain practice applying what you have just learned.

Skill Builder

Rule 1: Semicolon No Conjunction (NC)

Instructions: Place semicolons where needed in the following sentences. For each main clause, underline the subject once and the verb twice, for example:

> **Incorrect:** Addison arrived at 8 o'clock, she forgot the agenda.
>
> **Corrected:** Addison arrived at 8 o'clock; she forgot the agenda.

1. Miller will not approve our expense account she needs more documentation.

2. Ask Bryan for the report he said that he completed it yesterday.

3. Arrive on time to tomorrow's meeting bring both of your reports.

4. A laptop was left in the conference room Jason claimed it as his.

5. Recognize your mistakes offer apologies as needed.

Note: See page 88 for the answer key to the above sentences.

Rule 2: Semicolon Bridge (BR)

Use a semicolon before and a comma after an adverbial conjunction that acts as a bridge between two independent clauses.

This semicolon rule corresponds to the comma parenthetical expression (PE) rule. With the comma parenthetical expression, an adverbial conjunction (shown in italics) interrupts one independent clause, for example:

Comma PE: Bob, *however*, will determine the fees.

Instead, the semicolon bridge rule involves two complete sentences, with an adverbial conjunction providing a bridge or transition between the two:

Semicolon BR: Bob will determine the fees; *however*, he is open to suggestions.

For those who avoided semicolons prior to working on this lesson, here is how the above sentence might have been punctuated:

Incorrect: Bob will determine the fees, *however*, he is open to suggestions.

In the above example, by placing a comma where a semicolon (or period) would belong, your result is a run-on sentence.

Here are more examples of the semicolon bridge rule (with the adverbial conjunctions shown in italics):

Lidia wrote the grant; *therefore*, she should be on the committee.

The grant was accepted; *as a result*, we will receive funding.

You should call their office; *however*, (you) do not leave a message.

Now that you have reviewed this rule, can you see how you may have needed to use semicolons instead of commas at times? Do the practice exercises below before going on to the next semicolon rule.

Skill Builder

Rule 2: Semicolon Bridge (BR)

Instructions: Place commas and semicolons where needed in the following sentences. For each main clause, underline the subject once and the verb twice, for example:

> **Incorrect:** Feranda left, however, she forgot her briefcase.
>
> **Corrected:** Feranda left; however, she forgot her briefcase.

1. Carol suggested the topic fortunately Carlos agreed.

2. The project management team offered assistance however their time was limited.

3. Ken compiled the data therefore Mary crunched it.

4. The numbers turned out well as a result our new budget was accepted.

5. Roger ran in the marathon unfortunately he was unable to finish.

Note: See page 88 for the answer key to the above sentences.

Rule 3: Semicolon Because of Comma (BC)

When a clause needs major and minor separations, use semicolons for major breaks and commas for minor breaks.

This semicolon rule differs from the other two rules because it does not involve a "full stop"; in other words, this rule does not follow the "semicolon in place of period" rule of thumb that you learned earlier.

In addition, the need for the semicolon because of comma (BC) rule occurs less frequently than the other types of semicolons because most sentences do not call for both major and minor breaks. Even though this semicolon rule will not be used as often as the others, it is nonetheless necessary at times.

Apply this rule when listing a series of city and state names, for example:

Semicolon BC: Joni will travel to Dallas, Texas; Buffalo, New York; and Boston, Massachusetts.

Since the state names need commas around them, reading the above sentence without semicolons would be confusing:

Incorrect: Joni will travel to Dallas, Texas, Buffalo, New York, and Boston, Massachusetts.

Also apply this rule when listing a series of names and titles:

Semicolon BC: The committee members are Jeremy Smith, director of finance; Marjorie Lou Kirk, assistant vice president; Carson Michaels, accountant; and Malory Willbrook, broker.

A more complicated example would include major and minor clauses within a sentence:

Semicolon BC: Milicent asked for a raise; and since she was a new employee, I deferred to Jackson's opinion.

Semicolon BC: Dr. Jones suggested the procedure; but I was unable to help, so he asked Dr. Bender.

Skill Builder

Rule 3: Semicolon Because of Commas (BC)

Instructions: Place commas and semicolons where needed in the following sentences. In each main clause, underline the subject once and the verb twice.

Incorrect:	Gladys lived in Boise, Idaho, Biloxi, Mississippi, and Tallahassee, Florida.
Corrected:	<u>Gladys</u> <u><u>lived</u></u> in Boise, Idaho; Biloxi, Mississippi; and Tallahassee, Florida.

1. Please include Rupert Adams CEO Madeline Story COO and Mark Coleman executive president.
2. By next week I will have traveled to St. Louis Missouri Chicago Illinois and Burlington Iowa.
3. Mike applied for jobs in Honolulu Hawaii Sacramento California and Santa Fe New Mexico.
4. Your application was received yesterday but when I reviewed it information was missing.
5. You can resubmit your application today and since my office will review it you can call me tomorrow for the results.

Note: See page 88 for the answer key to the above sentences.

Writing Style: Punctuation and Flow

Now that you are using punctuation correctly, also consider how punctuation affects your writing style: punctuation packages your words, leading to a rhythm that affects the tone of your writing.

Writing generally does not flow well when it consists of short, choppy sentences. However, at times short, choppy sentences create a desired dramatic effect, as in the following:

Conan arrived late today. He resigned.

Most of the time, however, you want to reduce the choppy effect that short sentences can create; semicolons help you achieve that by connecting short sentences that are related. In addition to the semicolon, you have other tools: use a subordinate conjunction or adverbial conjunction to draw a connection for the reader, thereby aiding the flow of the writing. Consider the following example:

Matt offered the condo at a lower price; he needs to relocate.

In the above example, connecting the independent clauses with a semicolon does not necessarily reduce the choppy effect of the writing. The reader needs a transitional word to build a bridge between the "cause and the effect." Here are some ways to solve the problem through the use of conjunctions:

Matt offered the condo at a lower price since he needs to relocate.

Matt offered the condo at a lower price because he needs to relocate.

Matt offered the condo at a lower price; unfortunately, he needs to relocate.

In each example above, the conjunction smoothed out the flow of the writing. By giving the reader a transitional word, the reader can more readily draw a connection between the meanings of the two clauses.

Now that you are able to use commas and semicolons correctly, set higher expectations of your skills: experiment with punctuation and conjunctions until you gain a sense of how to use them more effectively. Punctuation is one more tool to help you connect with your reader and get your message across: work with punctuation until you understand how it helps you express your voice.

Workshop Activity

Instructions: Work with a partner to complete the Skills Workshop. After you complete Worksheets 1, 2, 3, you will be ready to move on to Lesson 6: The Colon, the Dash, and the Ellipses.

Recap

Below is a summary of the three semicolon rules that you have learned in this lesson.

Semicolon Rules

Rule 1: Semicolon No Conjunction (NC)

Use a semicolon to separate two independent clauses that are joined without a conjunction.

Rule 2: Semicolon Bridge (BR)

Use a semicolon before and a comma after an adverbial conjunction that bridges two independent clauses.

Rule 3: Semicolon Because of Comma (BC)

When a clause needs major and minor separations, use semicolons for major breaks and commas for minor breaks.

Writing Workshop

Activity A. Writing Practice

Instructions: Read and analyze an article that discusses a goal that you want to achieve. What is the overall purpose of the article or its "thesis." What audience does the article target? Is the tone emotional or persuasive? If so, why? Finally, identify and explain two or three key points that the article makes. Write a paragraph to summarize each key point: in other words, what did you learn from the article that you will apply?

For a more formal start to your essay, give the author's first and last name, the title of the article, and then the purpose of the article, as shown below:

> In John Smith's article entitled "Write for Results," Smith argues (or asserts or reveals, etc.) that writing is the most critical skill for career success today.

Activity B. Journal

Instructions: What is your favorite color? Can you describe it? What things or feelings does it remind you of? For example, "The color green reminds me of summer and trees as well as money and my favorite shirt . . . ." If you have trouble getting started, you can use the following template:

My favorite color is _____, and it reminds me of _____.
(Write two to three paragraphs.)

Are you following the 2 x 4 approach, writing two pages, four times a week? Do not let yourself fall behind. Have you had any recent insights that you would like to write about?

Skills Workshop

Worksheet 1. Semicolon No Conjunction (NC) and Comma Conjunction (CONJ)

Instructions: Place commas and semicolons where needed in the following sentences. For each main clause, underline the subject once and the verb twice. In addition, identify the reason for each mark of punctuation, for example:

Incorrect: Mark invited me to the Green Tree reception I accepted his offer.

Corrected: Mark invited me to the Green Tree reception; I accepted his offer. NC

1.   The Green Tree reception was elegant it was a black tie event.

2. I arrived early to the event and everyone seemed very friendly.

3. The group expressed concern about the environment they all wanted to see immediate and substantial change.

4. The keynote speaker shared new data about climate change everyone listened attentively to the entire speech.

5. Mark suggested that we join the group so he inquired about the requirements for membership.

6. Membership required participation at various levels both of us were already overextended.

7. The group's mission appealed to me and I was excited about getting involved.

8. Mark thought it over for a while yet he was still not ready to commit.

9. The environmental movement grows every year but more help is urgently needed.

10. Mark finally agreed to join the group my excitement tipped him in the right direction.

11. Their first meeting is next week and we both plan to go to it.

12. I will volunteer for the same project that Mark works on working together is fun.

Worksheet 2. Semicolon Bridge (BR) and Comma Parenthetical (PAR)

Instructions: Place commas and semicolons where needed in the following sentences. For each main clause, underline the subject once and the verb twice. In addition, identify the reason for each mark of punctuation, for example:

Incorrect: Technology advances every day in fact most people have trouble keeping up with it.

Corrected: Technology advances every day; in fact, most people have trouble keeping up with it. BR

1. Keeping up with technology can however make a difference in your career.

2. Different generations have different sorts of issues with technology for example younger people have an easier time learning new technology.

3. Today's young people used computers throughout their schooling consequently they find technology a natural part of their world.

4. Older generations however didn't have access to technology in school.

5. They needed to learn how to use computers and software on the job as a result many consider themselves "technologically illiterate."

6. It is never too late though to learn how to use a computer.

7. Taking classes at a local college can sometimes be inconvenient however you can research training opportunities online.

8. Online classes make learning convenient for example you can learn while you are in your own home office.

9. Most companies offer in-house training fortunately their employees stay at the cutting edge of technology.

10. Getting a job at a major corporation therefore helps ensure that you will keep your skills up-to-date.

11. Take advantage of all opportunities to build your skills for example keep an eye on your college and company newsletters.

12. Computer classes and other sorts of career classes are offered however only the most motivated enroll in them.

Worksheet 3. Semicolon and Comma Review

Instructions: Place commas and semicolons where needed in the following sentences. For each main clause, underline the subject once and the verb twice. In addition, identify the reason for each mark of punctuation, for example:

Incorrect: Technology advances every day in fact most people have trouble keeping up with it.

Corrected: Technology advances every day; in fact, most people have trouble keeping up with it. BR

1. Finding a job is challenging however certain pointers can help make it easier.

2. You need to stay abreast of job search techniques fortunately best practices are easily accessible.

3. You must do your research college placement offices, online sources, and books provide an abundance of information.

4. A colleague of mine applied for jobs in such diverse locations as Buffalo New York Oak Brook Illinois and Phoenix Arizona.

5. Searching for a job online expedited the project however the job search was still demanding and taxing.

6. Most people don't like extended periods of not knowing where their future lies facing the unknown creates anxiety.

7. Staying busy is a key to managing a job search the more you do the better you will feel about yourself and your opportunities.

8. Spend as much time as you can on your job search in fact some people say that you need to treat "finding a job as a full-time a job."

9. Print a business card that gives your contact information update your resume.

10. Consider networking as one of your primary sources for leads therefore make a list of people whom you can contact and events that you can attend.

11. Stay positive about your future something good will happen when you least expect it.

12. Securing your dream job is not an end to the process in today's world business changes constantly.

13. Doing a great job does not ensure that you will stay with a company forever keeping your skills up-to-date is your best insurance for a secure future.

14. Keep your finances flexible save regularly so that you have a nest egg to finance your next job search.

15. With hard work and a little luck, you will achieve your dreams you deserve the best!

Keys to Lesson 5 Skill Builders

Key to Rule 1: Semicolon No Conjunction (NC)

1. <u>Miller</u> <u>will</u> not <u>approve</u> our expense account; <u>she</u> <u>needs</u> more documentation.

2. (<u>You</u>) <u>Ask</u> Bryan for the report; <u>he</u> <u>said</u> that it was completed yesterday.

3. (<u>You</u>) <u>Arrive</u> on time to tomorrow's meeting; (<u>you</u>) <u>bring</u> both of your reports.

4. A <u>laptop</u> <u>was</u> <u>left</u> in the conference room; <u>Jason</u> <u>claimed</u> it as his.

5. (<u>You</u>) <u>Recognize</u> your mistakes; (<u>you</u>) <u>offer</u> apologies as needed.

Key to Rule 2: Semicolon Bridge (BR)

1. <u>Carol</u> <u>suggested</u> the topic; fortunately, <u>Carlos</u> <u>agreed</u>.

2. The project management <u>team</u> <u>offered</u> assistance; however, their <u>time</u> <u>was</u> limited.

3. <u>Ken</u> <u>compiled</u> the data; therefore, <u>Mary</u> <u>crunched</u> it.

4. The <u>numbers</u> <u>turned out</u>* well; as a result, our new <u>budget</u> <u>was</u> <u>accepted</u>.

5. <u>Roger</u> <u>ran</u> in the marathon; unfortunately, <u>he</u> <u>was</u> unable to finish.

* "Turned out" is a verb phrase.

Key to Rule 3: Semicolon Because of Commas (BC)

1. (<u>You</u>) Please <u>include</u> Rupert Adams, CEO; Madeline Story, COO; and Mark Coleman, executive president.

2. By next week <u>I</u> <u>will</u> <u>have</u> <u>traveled</u> to St. Louis, Missouri; Chicago, Illinois; and Burlington, Iowa.

3. <u>Mike</u> <u>applied</u> for jobs in Honolulu, Hawaii; Sacramento, California; and Santa Fe, New Mexico.

4. Your <u>application</u> <u>was</u> <u>received</u> yesterday; but when <u>I</u> <u>reviewed</u> it, <u>information</u> <u>was</u> missing.

5. <u>You</u> <u>can</u> <u>resubmit</u> your application today; and since my <u>office</u> <u>will</u> <u>review</u> it, <u>you</u> <u>can</u> <u>call</u> me tomorrow for the results.

6

The Colon,
the Dash, and the Ellipses

In the process of mastering the use of commas and semicolons, you have established a firm foundation in core principles of grammar. Though you may not yet see the connection, you have also taken steps to control your writing style.

One reason that writing seems so difficult for most people is that they are trying to make a multitude of decisions all at once. The principles you learn here will allow you to make decisions about mechanics without effort, freeing your energies to create a writing style that is reader-friendly and clear.

Now you can add some variety and a few more layers of depth by learning about the colon, the dash, and the ellipses. In fact, this lesson and the rest of the topics in this book may seem like fun compared to the hard work you have already put in to improving your skills.

Let's start with the colon because it has unique and versatile functions.

The Colon

In general, the colon alerts readers that information will be illustrated, making the colon a strong mark of punctuation that commands attention.

The colon is used for the following purposes:

1. After salutations of business letters (and formal e-mail messages).
2. At the end of one sentence when the following sentence illustrates it.
3. At the end of a sentence to alert the reader that a list follows.
4. After words such as *Note* or *Caution*.

Each of these categories is explained below.

1. Colons after Salutations. The most common use of a colon is after the salutation in a business letter, which is the most formal type of written communication. Only when you write a letter to a personal friend should you relax that tradition, using a comma instead of a colon. Here are some examples of salutations using a colon:

Dear Mr. Jones: Dear Dr. Wilson: Dear Professor:

Dear Jorge: Dear Mia: Robert:

Notice that even when using the recipient's first name, the colon is appropriate. The above salutations could also be used with e-mail if the message were formal, such as an inquiry for a job. However, for the most part, business professionals use a comma after the salutation of an e-mail as in the following:

Dear Janet,   Jack,   Hi Carolyn,

The one mark of punctuation that you would *never* use for a salutation is the semicolon; however, some writers mistakenly use it, for example:

Incorrect: Dear Charles;

Correct: Dear Charles:

Correct: Dear Charles,

Now let's examine how to use the colon to add variety to your writing style.

2. Colons after Sentences. You have probably noticed that a colon is used to introduce lists, but have you noticed a colon sometimes occurs at the end of one sentence when the following sentence illustrates it?

Using a colon to illustrate a complete sentence is probably the colon's least common use, but possibly its most powerful use. This type of colon use adds a nice dimension to writing style: the writing conveys the message in a slightly more emphatic way. Here are some examples of one sentence introducing another:

Update your report by Friday: The accrediting commission's site visit is next week.

The colon is a strong mark of punctuation: it draws the reader's attention.

Johnson Ecology accepted our proposal: we start on Monday.

In general, the first word of the independent clause following a colon should be in lower case. However, capitalize the first word if you are placing special emphasis on that second clause or the second clause is a formal rule, as shown below:[1]

Here is the principle that applies: Colons can be used in place of a period when the sentence that follows illustrates the one that precedes it.

Update your report by Friday: The accrediting commission's site visit is next week.

When you use a colon to illustrate a sentence, use it sparingly. If you overuse the colon in this way, readers get tired of it—similar to the overuse of exclamation points. While there is no hard and fast rule, limit yourself to no more than one or two colons per page used this way.

If you have never used a colon in this way, try it. Once you do, you may enjoy having this new and exciting punctuation alternative. Experiment by writing a sentence or two on the lines below to illustrate this principle.

_____

_____

_____

_____

3. Colons to Illustrate Lists. Using the colon to illustrate a list of words or phrases generally requires using words such as "these," "here," "the following," or "as follows" within a complete sentence. Here are some examples:

> These are the materials to bring to the meeting: your annual report and current data.
>
> Bring the following identification: driver's license, social security card, and current utility bill.
>
> Here are writing samples that you can use: Myers, Jones, and Riley.

However, do not use a colon after an incomplete sentence, for example:

| **Incorrect:** | The items you need to bring are: a tent, a sleeping bag, and a flashlight. |
| **Corrected:** | The items you need to bring are a tent, a sleeping bag, and a flashlight. |

| **Incorrect:** | This package includes: a stapler and 3-hole paper punch. |
| **Corrected:** | This package includes a stapler and 3-hole paper punch. |

Also notice that the colon can be used after the word "for example" to alert the reader that an example follows.

4. Colons After *Note* or *Caution* Use a colon after a word of caution or instruction, for example:

> Note: All meetings are cancelled on Friday.
>
> Caution: Do not use the staircase.

If a complete sentence follows *Note* or *Caution*, capitalize the first word, as shown above.

Skill Builder

The Colon

Instructions: Place colons where needed in the following sentences.

Incorrect: The materials we need are: blankets, water, and cell phones.

Corrected: The materials we need are blankets, water, and cell phones.

1. I have some exciting news for you, Jeremy proposed on Friday.
2. Note, the office is closed on Monday to honor the Martin Luther King holiday.
3. The supplies we need are as follows; markers copy paper and staplers.
4. Giorgio said that we need: cereal, soy milk, and bananas.
5. Here is what you should do, complete the inventory list and then work on the schedule.

Note: See page 102 for the answer key to the above sentences.

The Dash

The dash is the most versatile mark of punctuation, at times replacing the comma, the semicolon, the period, and even the colon.

The dash adds energy, making information that follows one dash or that falls between two dashes stand out. Though the dash can be used in formal documents, it is most often used in informal communications. However, do not overuse the dash. When overused, the dash gives the impression that the writer is "speaking" in a choppy and haphazard fashion. Limit yourself with the dash to no more than one or two per page or e-mail message.

Here are some examples using the dash:

Bob called on Friday—he said he'd arrive by noon today.

Thanks—your package arrived right before our meeting.

Feranda Wilson—our new executive VP—will host the event.

Though the dash is different from the hyphen, the hyphen is used to create the dash. Here are two ways to create a dash using hyphens:

1. Use two hyphens without a space before, between, after them; some software will create an *em* dash, as illustrated in the sentences above.

2. Use two hyphens, but this time place a space before and after the hyphens to create an *en* dash, as follows:

> Marie Clair invited us to the opening – I am so pleased!

The em dash is the more traditional choice. However, if you work for a company, check your company policy manual to see if the manual states a preference—some companies state a preference so that corporate communications remain consistent.

Once again, overusing dashes is similar to overusing colons or exclamation points. Writers enjoy using them, but readers tire of them easily. Thus, hold yourself back and use them sparingly. However, if you have never used a dash in your writing, try it. Dashes definitely add energy and are fun to use.

Skill Builder

The Dash

Instructions: Place dashes where needed in the following sentences.

Incorrect: Mark scheduled the meeting, how could I refuse to go?

Corrected: Mark scheduled the meeting—how could I refuse to go?

1. Margie called on Friday George is home!

2. Mike's parents are visiting he invited me to have dinner with them.

3. Helen Jones the new CEO asked me to join her team.

4. Call if you need anything I'm always here to support you.

5. Give as much as you can to that charity it's a good cause.

Note: See page 102 for the answer key to the above sentences.

The Ellipses

Ellipses is the plural form for *ellipsis marks.* Ellipses indicate that information is missing, thereby removing an otherwise awkward gap.

In formal documents, ellipses allow writers to adapt quotations by leaving out less relevant information, making the main idea stand out. In informal documents, ellipses allow writers to jump from one idea to another without entirely completing their thoughts. Ellipses also allow the writer to convey a sense of uncertainty without coming right out and stating it.

- Ellipsis marks consist of three periods with a space before, between, and after each one, for example:

  This doesn't make sense to me . . . let me know what you think.

- Some software programs create ellipses when you space once, type three periods in a row, and then space once again, as follows:

  Vic was not pleased ... he will call back later.

Before using the "unspaced" ellipses described above, check to make sure that it is acceptable practice within the domain you are submitting your work, as the unspaced ellipses may not be acceptable.

Many writers are unsure of how to display ellipses and end up using two, four, or five periods; even worse, some writers vary the number of periods they use each time, not realizing that rules surround the use of ellipses.

The only time a fourth period would be used is when the missing information is at the end of the sentence in a formal quotation, for example:

> The topics taught include self-awareness, in the sense of recognizing feelings and building a vocabulary for them, and seeing the links between thoughts, feelings, and reactions . . . .[1]

As with dashes, use ellipsis marks sparingly, even for informal use. However, whenever you use ellipsis marks, display them correctly.

Skill Builder

Ellipses

Instructions: Use ellipsis marks to show how to adjust the following quotations while retaining the key meaning of each quote; for example:

Original Quote by John F. Kennedy:

"The great enemy of the truth is very often not the lie—deliberate, contrived and dishonest, but the myth, persistent, persuasive, and unrealistic. Belief in myths allows the comfort of opinion without the discomfort of thought.[2]

Abbreviated Quote:

"The great enemy of the truth is very often not the lie . . . . Belief in myths allows the comfort of opinion without the discomfort of thought."

1. Original Quote by Albert Einstein:

"The important thing is not to stop questioning. Curiosity has its own reason for existing. One cannot help but be in awe when he contemplates the mysteries of eternity, of life, of the marvelous structure of reality. It is enough if one tries merely to comprehend a little of this mystery every day. Never lose a holy curiosity." [3]

Abbreviated Quote:

_____

_____

_____

_____

2. Original Quote by Victor Frankl:

"Don't aim at success—the more you aim at it and make it a target, the more you are going to miss it. For success, like happiness, cannot be pursued; it must ensue, and it only does so as the unintended side-effect of one's dedication to a cause greater than oneself or as the by product of one's surrender to a person other than oneself. Happiness must happen, and the same holds true for success: you have to let it happen by not caring about it. I want you to listen to what your conscience commands you to do and go on to carry it out to the best of your knowledge. Then you will live to see that in the long run—in the long run, I say!—success will follow you precisely because you had *forgotten* to think of it."[4]

Abbreviated Quote:

_____

_____

_____

_____

Note: See page 102 for the answer key to the above quotations.

Workshop Activity

Instructions: Work with a partner to complete the Skills Workshop. After you complete Worksheets 1 and 2, you will be ready to work on Lesson 7: Capitalization and Number Usage.

Recap

Below is a summary of the colon, dash, and ellipses: three marks that can give your writing variety and flair, as long as they are not overused.

➤ The colon illustrates information that follows it; here are some basic guidelines:

- Use the colon at the end of one sentence when the following sentence illustrates it.

- Use the colon after a complete sentence that includes words such as "these" or "the following" to indicate that a list follows.

- Use the colon after the words "Note" and "Caution"; if a complete sentence follows the colon, capitalize the first word of that sentence.

➤ The dash emphasizes information that falls between two dashes or after one dash; create a dash as follows:

- Use two hyphens without spaces before, between, or after them to create an em dash.
- Use two hyphens with a space before (but not between) and after them to create an en dash.

➤ The ellipses fill gaps and allow the reader to express uncertainty; create ellipses as follows:

- Use three periods and include a space before, between, and after each period.
- Use a fourth period at the end of sentence.

Writing Workshop

Activity A. Writing Practice

Instructions: Identify an historical figure whom you respect. Go to the Internet and find a long quotation by that person. Google the following: "quotations by (insert the name)." Several quotation sites should become available. Use ellipsis marks to shorten your quote, thereby emphasizing the key point of the original quotation.

Activity B. Journal

Instructions: Experiment using dashes, colons, and ellipses as you write your journals this week. Go back to some of your earlier journal entries and notice how you used punctuation. Choose one entry from the first or second week that you started your journal; correct and revise the punctuation of that journal entry. Write one journal this week that discusses how your thinking about punctuation has changed . . . or not changed.

Skills Workshop

Worksheet 1. Colons and Dashes

Instructions: Place colons and dashes where needed in the following sentences. Note: Your answers may vary as these marks of punctuation are often interchangeable.

Incorrect:	Call if you need me, I will support you 100 percent in this venture.
Corrected:	Call if you need me: I will support you 100 percent in this venture.
Corrected:	Call if you need me—I will support you 100 percent in this venture.

1. Jeremy suggested several changes add more personnel, start offering carry out, and remain open on Sundays but I disagree with him on all points.

2. Here's what you need to look out for; their Eastern branch office does not have a sales manager.

3. If you ask for a lower price even one that is not unreasonable they will not know how to handle your request.

4. Caution, do not use this equipment in temperatures below freezing.

5. Note, Friday is a holiday and our offices will be closed.

6. Sean refused to share the plan he simply wouldn't answer my questions.

7. These are the people you should interview, Eddie Stone Fred Harris and Bill Janulewicz.

8. All of them especially Bill Janulewicz are extremely knowledgeable of our products.

9. Remain positive, you do not yet know how they will respond to your offer.

10. I received a call from McCracken's CEO, yes their CEO, to join the marketing team.

Worksheet 2. Colons, Dashes, and Ellipses

Instructions: Place colons, dashes, and ellipses where needed in the following sentences. Note: Your answers may vary as these marks of punctuation are sometimes interchangeable.

Incorrect: Think about it, the answer will become apparent.

Corrected: Think about it . . . the answer will become apparent.

Corrected: Think about it—the answer will become apparent.

1. Scot said that we shouldn't worry .....the product research team will meet tomorrow.

2. Note the following, more people need to travel today but fewer people enjoy it.

3. The Mercer group became involved of their own accord I didn't invite them.

4. Follow your passions you will create a career that you enjoy.

5. I couldn't understand what John said, "The biggest seller is."

6. Send your resume directly to the CEO he is expecting to hear from you.

7. Toni and Joe bought the company they are ecstatic.

8. You know what I mean things just aren't working out.

9. Keep your spirits up you will have another opportunity soon.

10. Read between the lines watch the body language.

Keys to Lesson 6 Skill Builders

Key to Practice with Colons

1. I have some exciting news for you: Jeremy proposed on Friday.
2. Note: The office is closed on Monday to honor the Martin Luther King holiday.
3. The supplies we need are as follows: markers, copy paper, and staplers.
4. Giorgio said that we need cereal, soy milk, and bananas.
5. Here is what you should do: complete the inventory list and then work on the schedule. (Or: Complete . . .)

Key to Practice with Dashes

1. Margie called on Friday—George is home!
2. Mike's parents are in town—he invited me to have dinner with them.
3. Helen Jones—the new CEO—asked me to join her team.
4. Call if you need anything—I'm always here to support you.
5. Give as much as you can to that charity—it's a good cause.

Key to Practice with Ellipses (Answers will vary).

1. **Abbreviated Albert Einstein Quote:** "The important thing is not to stop questioning . . . Never lose a holy curiosity."
2. **Abbreviated Victor Frankl Quote:** "Don't aim at success—the more you aim at it and make it a target, the more you are going to miss it . . . success will follow you precisely because you had *forgotten* to think to it."

Lesson 6 End Notes

1. William A. Sabin, *The Gregg Reference Manual*, Tenth Edition, McGraw-Hill/Irwin, Burr Ridge, 2005, page 52.
2. Daniel Goleman, *Emotional Intelligence*, Bantam Books, New York, 1995, page 268.
3. John F. Kennedy quotation accessed at www.quotationspage.com/quotes/J_F_Kennedy on January 24, 2008.
4. Albert Einstein quotation accessed at http://quotationspage.com/quotes/Albert_Einstein on January 25, 2008.
5. Victor Frankl, *Man's Search for Meaning*, Beacon Press, Boston, 2006, page xiv-xv.

7

Capitalization and Number Usage

Capitalization decisions can be confusing. Some words and titles sound so official, they simply *must* be capitalized. However, you may be surprised to learn that most of the time those official-sounding words and titles are not capitalized: they are not proper nouns. But why waste time and energy guessing. The first part of this lesson gives you the information you need to make most capitalization decisions.

Then there is number usage. When you stop to decide whether to spell out a number in words or to use numerals, you waste time. A few basic number rules will make a big difference in how you use numbers in your writing.

This lesson answers the most common questions about capitalization and number usage so that you can make effective decisions. However, when you come across more complicated situations than the basic rules here can solve, turn to a detailed reference manual such as *The Gregg Reference Manual*.[1]

Capitalization

Many writers are naïve about capitalization. Instead of respecting the basics and staying safe, they start capitalizing all sorts of words for which there is no logical rationale. You may have seen this, or maybe you have this inclination. It is an easy problem to solve. Let's start with the following:

When in doubt, do not capitalize.

In other words, unless you know for sure that a word should be capitalized, leave the word in lower case.

Here are the two major categories of words that should be capitalized:

- Proper nouns
- First words of sentences, poems, displayed lists, and so on

The challenge then becomes knowing which words are proper nouns and which are common nouns. Let's start by taking a look at the difference between the two and then identifying some of the most common types of capitalization errors.

Proper Nouns and Common Nouns

To avoid capitalizing common nouns, you must first learn the difference between common nouns and proper nouns. The chart below helps illuminate some of the differences:

Proper Noun	Common Noun
John Wilson	name, person, friend, business associate
Wilson Corporation	company, corporation, business
Southlake Mall	shopping, stores, shops
New York	state, city
Italy	country

Words derived from proper nouns become proper adjectives and are also capitalized:

Proper Noun	Derivative or Proper Adjective
England	English language
Spain	Spanish 101
Italy	Italian cookware
French	French class

Names are proper nouns, and that includes the names of people as well as the names of places and things, such as the following:[2]

Titles of literary and artistic works	Chicago Tribune, the Bible
Periods of time and historical events	Great Depression
Imaginative names and nicknames	Big Apple
Brand and trade names	IBM, 3M, Xerox copier
Points of the compass	the North, the South, the Southwest *(when they refer to specific geographic regions)*
Place names	Coliseum, Eiffel Tower
Organization names	National Business Education Association
Words derived from proper nouns	English, South American
Days of the week, months, and holidays	Thanksgiving, Christmas, Chanukah

Articles, Conjunctions, and Prepositions

Not every word of a title is capitalized, and the types words in question are articles, conjunctions, and prepositions. Let's start by clarifying what to look for:

Articles:	the, a, an
Conjunctions:	and, but, or, for, nor
Prepositions:	between, to, at, among, from, over

Here are rules about capitalizing articles, conjunctions, and prepositions:

1. Capitalize any of these words when it is the first word of a title or subtitle.
2. As for prepositions, some sources say to capitalize them when they consist of four letters, others say to capitalize them when they consist of five or more letters; to be safe, capitalize prepositions only when they are the first or last word of a title or subtitle.

Here are some examples:

The University of Chicago

Pride and Prejudice

Writing from the Core: A Grammatical Writer

In the above, the word "the" is part of the official name of The University of Chicago. Other organizations incorporate the word "the" into their official name as well, so *when in doubt, check it out.*

First Words

As already seen above, the *first word* is given special designation. Here is a list of the kinds of categories to be on the lookout for, ensuring that you capitalize the first word: [3]

Sentences

Poems

Direct quotations that are complete sentences

Independent questions within a sentence

Items displayed in a list or outline

Salutations and complimentary closings

Also capitalize the first word of a complete sentence that follows a word of caution or instruction, such as *Note* or *Caution.*

Hyphenated Terms

At times, you will need to determine how to capitalize hyphenated words, such as e-mail, long-term, up-to-date, and so on. Here are some guidelines:

- Capitalize parts of the hyphenated word that are proper nouns:

  If I receive your information by mid-December, you will qualify for the training.

- Capitalize the first word of a hyphenated word when it is the first word of the sentence, for example:

  E-mail is the preferred mode of communication.

  Mid-January is when the quarterly reports are expected.

- Capitalize each word of a hyphenated term used in a title (except short prepositions and conjunctions, as previously noted), for example:

Up-to-Date Reports	Mid-July Conference
E-Mail Guidelines	Long-Term Outlook

Let's look at titles and terms associated with organizations, for which capitalization decisions can also be challenging.

Organizational Titles and Terms

Most people believe that their work title is a proper noun, but professional titles are *not* proper nouns. Here are some rules to follow:

- Capitalize a professional title when it precedes the name.
- Do not capitalize a professional title when it follows the name.
- Capitalize organizational terms in your own company (but not necessarily other companies), such as the names of departments and committees.

Here are some examples:

Incorrect: John Smith, Vice President, will be meeting with the Finance Department.

Correct: John Smith, vice president, will be meeting with the Finance Department.

Correct: Vice President John Smith will be meeting with the Finance Department.

You may capitalize organizational terms from other companies to show special importance. In addition, the titles of high government officials are capitalized:

Correct: The President had a meeting in the West Wing of the White House.

Finally, let's examine two types of capitalization errors that are so pervasive that they merit special attention.

Two Common Capitalization Errors

You will have come a long way with capitalization if you stop capitalizing words randomly and follow the rules discussed above. However, the following two common types of errors fit into a special class of their own.

Error No. 1: Leaving the pronoun *I* in lower case. The personal pronoun *I* is a proper noun and should always be represented in upper case. Partly due to text messaging, the problem of leaving the personal pronoun *I* in lower case has escalated, for example:

Incorrect: A friend asked me if i could help, so i said that i would.

Correct: A friend asked if I could help, so I said that I would.

Whenever you use the pronoun *I*, capitalize it; and that includes its use in e-mail messages.

Error No. 2: Using all UPPER CASE or all lower case. Another type of error that occurs, especially with e-mail, is typing everything in either lower case or upper case. Neither version is correct, but putting everything in upper case has earned the reputation that the writer is shouting. The truth is, the writer is not necessarily shouting. Most of the time, when writers use all caps, it is because they are unsure about writing decisions; putting the message in all caps (inaccurately) seems like an easy way out.

When writers put everything in lower case, it often reflects a tradition within certain professional niches. For example, some computer professionals communicate primarily with other technical professionals in lower case. When communicating to professionals outside of their inner circle, these technical professionals continue to leave their words in lower case. For these professionals, adjusting to their audience is the key: Distinguish who is within your circle and who is not and then adapt accordingly.

Global Communication and the Rules

All writers need to adapt to their audience to the best of their ability. Rules such as the ones discussed throughout this book take the guessing out of written communication; however, they also do something more important. Rules create standards so that everyone can understand the meaning of the message, reducing confusion and misunderstanding among readers.

This advice is more timely now than ever because most professional communication can be considered global communication. People for whom English is a second language find deviations from the rules difficult to understand. Using a second language according to the standard rules is hard enough, let alone trying to adapt to all of the idiosyncrasies that sprout up as a result of misuse of the language.

Skill Builder

Capitalization

Instructions: In the following paragraph, correct errors in capitalization.

Next year the President of my Company will provide a Financial Incentive for all employees, and i plan to participate in it. Jack Edwards, Vice President of Finance, will administer the plan. Everyone in my Department is looking forward to having the opportunity to save more. A Pamphlet entitled, "Financial Incentives For Long-term Savings" will describe the plan and be distributed next Week. If the Pamphlet has not arrived by friday, i will check with the Vice President's office to find out the details.

Note: See page 122 for the answer key to the above sentences.

Number Usage

Many writers, unaware of number rules, do not even stop to consider how to represent numbers. Other writers, aware that rules exist but unsure of the details, seek every possible way to represent numbers, thinking that they will be right at least some of the time.

The only way to break the confusion is to learn the rules; and unfortunately, the rules can seem complex at times. For example, the first number rule states the following:

Write numbers under ten as words,

but write numbers above ten as figures.

After this basic rule, every additional rule is some form of exception to it. In fact, the advice of *The Gregg Reference Manual* is that all numbers can be represented as figures—including those under ten—when the writer wants the numbers to stand out.

Learn the number rules—they are not that difficult. Beyond learning the rules, here is a recommendation for number usage based on the kinds of errors people make:

When in doubt, at least be consistent.

In other words, when you do not rely on the rules and instead "guess" (which is not recommended), at least represent numbers consistently as numerals or words throughout your writing—do not go back and forth, representing a number as a word in one place and then as a numeral in the next. However, you no longer need to be in doubt about number usage; here is a list of ten basic number rules: [2]

Rule 1: Numbers 1 through 10. Spell out numbers 1 through 10 within written text (unless you want the numbers displayed for quick reference); use numerals for numbers above 10.

Examples:

> I have ten reports to complete.
>
> Our department recognized 12 employees for providing excellent client service.

Rule 2: Numbers Beginning a Sentence. Spell out numbers beginning a sentence (however, avoid starting a sentence with a number whenever possible). If you start a sentence with a number, all numbers in that sentence must be spelled out.

Example:

> Sixteen new chairs and twelve new desks have arrived for offices on the fourth floor.

Rule 3: Related Numbers. Use the same form for related numbers within a sentence, with figures trumping words. In other words, if some numbers should be written in words (numbers under 10) and they are mixed with numbers that are above 10, write all numbers in figures.

Example:

> Bob brought 12 new individual clients and 5 new corporate accounts to our firm.

Rule 4: Unrelated Numbers. When two unrelated numbers come together, write the shorter number in words and the longer number in figures.

Example:

> Order 7 two-piece organizational units for my department.

Rule 5: Indefinite Numbers. Write indefinite numbers, such as thousands or hundreds, in words.

Example:

> You say that you have hundreds of problems, but in reality you could list them on one hand. Thousands of people support you.

Rule 6: Ordinal Numbers. Write ordinal numbers such as *first*, *second*, or *third*, and so on, in words.

Example:

> Lorraine lives on the fourteenth floor of the building at 900 North Lake Shore Drive.

Rule 7: Large Numbers. Numbers in the millions or higher can be written as a combination of figures and words if the number can be expressed as a whole number or as a whole number plus a simple fraction or a decimal amount.

Example:

> Our company extended their $1.5 million loan until April.

Rule 8. Fractions and Mixed Numbers. Write fractions as words with a hyphen between the numerator and denominator; write mixed numbers as figures.

Examples:

> Mix one-half of the dry ingredients before adding any liquid.

> Increase the amount of tomatoes to 2½ cups.

Rule 9. Percentages. Use figures for percentages and spell out the word *percent* unless the percentage is part of a table or technical material. Use the word *percentage* rather than *percent* when no number appears with it.

Examples:

> Chicago had a 10 percent decrease in crime last year.

> That lower percentage pleased the mayor.

Rule 10. Weights and Measures. Use figures for weights, measures, and other types of dimensions.

Examples:

> If you can lose 10 pounds, you are a better person than I am.

> The new room needs a carpet that is 10 feet by 15 feet.

In addition to these ten basic rules, dates and time have special guidelines, which we will look at next.

Dates and Time

Dates and time are commonly used in e-mail messages as well as other formal types of communication. Here are some basic guidelines:

- Use figures for dates and time on everything except formal invitations.
- Use the abbreviations a.m. and p.m. or the word *o'clock*, but not both.
- Spell out the names of days and months; in other words, do not abbreviate.
- For time on the hour, you may omit the :00 (unless you want to emphasize time on the hour).
- Use the ordinal ending for dates only when the day *precedes* the month.

Here are some examples:

Incorrect: The meeting is scheduled for Sept. 17th at 5 PM.

Correct: The meeting is scheduled for September 17 at 5 p.m.

Incorrect: Will you be available at 8:30 AM on the sixteenth of this month?

Correct: Will you be available at 8:30 a.m. on the 16th of this month?

Now let's review how to represent addresses and phone numbers.

Addresses and Phone Numbers

As with dates, parts of addresses should not be abbreviated. So before reviewing the rules for addresses and phone numbers, here is a guideline:

When in doubt, spell it out.

This guideline is not absolute: You can abbreviate parts of addresses when space is tight. However, do not abbreviate simply for the "convenience" of it.

Here are some rules for displaying addresses:

- Spell out parts of addresses: Do not abbreviate points of the compass such as *North* or *South* or words such as *avenue, street,* or *apartment.*
- Spell out street names *One* through *Ten.*
- Use figures for all house numbers except the number *One.*
- Add ordinal endings only when points of the compass (North, South, East, and West) are not included, for example: 1400 59th Street.
- Use two-letter state abbreviations.
- Leave one or two spaces between the two-letter state abbreviation and the zip code.

Here are some examples:

Mr. Alistair Cromby
One West Washington Avenue
St. Clair, MN 56080

Dr. Michael Jules
1214 79th Place, Suite 290
Chesterton, IN 46383

Mrs. Lionel Hershey
141 Meadow Lane South
Seattle, WA 92026

Ms. Lorel Lindsey
Associate Director
The Fine Arts Studio
500 North State Street, Suite 311
Chicago, IL 60611-6043

In general, the most specific part of an address is on the first line (the name of the addressee) and the broadest part of an address is on the last line (the name of the country or the name of the city and state), as shown above and below.

Mr. Lucas M. Matthews
72 O'Manda Road
Lake Olivia, VIC 3709
AUSTRALIA

Pierluigi e Sylvia D'Amici
Via Davide No. 1
00151 ROMA
I T A L I A

Here is a list of two-letter state abbreviations:

Alabama	AL	Montana	MT
Alaska	AK	Nebraska	NE
Arizona	AZ	Nevada	NV
Arkansas	AR	New Hampshire	NH
California	CA	New Jersey	NJ
Colorado	CO	New Mexico	NM
Connecticut	CT	New York	NY
Delaware	DE	North Carolina	NC
District of		North Dakota	ND
Columbia	DC	Ohio	OH
Florida	FL	Oklahoma	OK
Georgia	GA	Oregon	OR
Guam	GU	Pennsylvania	PA
Hawaii	HI	Puerto Rico	PR
Idaho	ID	Rhode Island	RI
Illinois	IL	South Carolina	SC
Indiana	IN	South Dakota	SD
Iowa	IA	Tennessee	TN
Kansas	KS	Texas	TX
Kentucky	KY	Utah	UT
Louisiana	LA	Vermont	VT
Maine	ME	Virgin Islands	VI
Maryland	MD	Virginia	VA
Massachusetts	MA	Washington	WA
Michigan	MI	West Virginia	WV
Minnesota	MN	Wisconsin	WI
Mississippi	MS	Wyoming	WY
Missouri	MO		

Display phone numbers by using a hyphen or period between parts.

Examples:

> You can reach me at 312-555-1212.
>
> I left the message at 502.555.1212.

Skill Builder

Numbers

Instructions: Make corrections to the way numbers are displayed in the following sentences.

> **Incorrect:** Reggie sent 10 copies of the report, but I received only 5.
>
> **Corrected:** Reggie sent ten copies of the report, but I received only five.

1. We are meeting on Jan. 5 at 10 AM at our offices on Lake St.

2. Call me on Mon. at (407) 555-1212.

3. Alex lists his address as 407 S. Maple St., Hobart, Ind. 46368.

4. We received 100s of calls about the job opening but only five resumes.

5. Purchase 12 laptops but only seven new printers for our department.

Note: See page 122 for the answer key to the above sentences.

Workshop Activity

Instructions: Work with a partner to complete the Skills Workshop. After you complete Worksheets 1 and 2, you will be ready to work on Lesson 8: Quotation Marks, Apostrophes, and Hyphens.

Recap

Below is a summary of the rules and guidelines you have learned in this lesson.

Capitalize the following:

> ➢ The personal pronoun *I*.

> ➢ Proper nouns and their derivatives, such as *England* and *English*.

> ➢ The first words of sentences, poems, displayed lists, and so on.

> ➢ Titles that precede a name, such as *President Gerry Smith*.

> ➢ The names of departments within your own organization.

Basic guidelines for representing numbers are as follows:

> ➢ Spell out numbers 1 through 10; use numbers if you want them to stand out.

> ➢ Use figures for numbers above 10.

> ➢ If numbers above and below 10 are in a sentence, use figures.

> ➢ Use numbers with the word *percent*, as in 25 percent.

> ➢ Use the word *percentage* (rather than *percent*) when it is used alone.

For dates, time, and addresses, do the following:

> ➢ Do not abbreviate: *When in doubt, spell it out*.

> ➢ Omit the :00 for time on the hour.

> ➢ Use a.m. and p.m. or o'clock, but do not use both.

> ➢ Use two-letter state abbreviations.

Writing Workshop

Activity A. Writing Practice

Instructions: As pre-work for updating your resume, compile the names and addresses of places you have worked, along with the dates of employment. Follow the guidelines given in this lesson for capitalization and number usage.

Activity B. Journal

Instructions: Are you following the 2 x 4 approach: writing two pages, four times a week? List three or four key points that you learned in this lesson—did any of the number or capitalization rules surprise you? What other changes are you making in your writing?

Skills Workshop

Worksheet 1. Capitalization and Number Usage

Instructions: Identify and correct the errors in the following e-mail message. You will find a variety of errors, including errors in capitalization and number usage as well as punctuation.

Dear Suzie;

THANK YOU for asking for more information about my work history. For 5 yrs. i worked for Rapid Communications as an Associate Manager in the Customer Service Dept. Here's info about how to contact my former boss Jake Roberts, Human Resources Director:

Mr Jake Roberts

Human Resources Dir.

Rapid Com.

14 N. Ogden Rd.

Burlington Iowa   52601

I look forward to hearing from you. You can reach me at (209) 555-1212 anytime between 9:00 AM and 5 o'clock PM Mon. thru Fri. until the end of Aug.

Best Regards,

Sylvia Marina

Worksheet 2. Number Usage and Capitalization

Instructions: The following sentences have errors in number usage and capitalization as well as other topics that you have covered in earlier lessons.

> **Incorrect:** Meet me in the lobby at 5;30 PM on Fri.
> **Corrected:** Meet me in the lobby at 5:30 p.m. on Friday.

1. The supply company delivered 5 copiers and 7 fax machines.
2. Ian, our new company Auditor, scheduled the meeting for Fri. Sept. 10 at 9AM.
3. Send the information to Lester Ostrom, 1213 W. Astor Pl., Chic., Ill. 60610.
4. Did you request twelve catalogs or only two?
5. The new budget for our computer purchase is $1,500,000 million.
6. We received 100s of calls, not 1000s as Jeffrey said.
7. Did you say i should meet you for lunch today at 12 o'clock PM or on Mon.?
8. Austin Roberts, Accounting Manager, gave me the instructions on how to complete my Taxes.
9. Vice president Tomas O'Rourke has a background in Law.
10. If the requirements call for 5 postings on 3 different days, allow yourself at least two hours a day to get the work done.
11. We had a ten percent decrease in our heating bill but a 50% increase in our water bill.
12. The closet is five ft. by eight ft.
13. If i can assist you with ½ of the mailing, let me know.
14. Eleven of the participants have arrived, but the remaining 12 are late.
15. Meet me on the 14th floor at 3:30 PM o'clock this afternoon.

Worksheet 3: Punctuation, Capitalization, and Number Usage

Instructions: Make corrections as needed in the following sentences.

Incorrect: On Mon. we will meet in the hawthorn room on the 4th floor but on Wed. we will meet in the Concord Rm. on the fifth fl.

Corrected: On Monday we will meet in the Hawthorn Room on the fourth floor, but on Wednesday we will meet in the Concord Room on the fifth floor.

1. Many colleges are offering online Degrees and you should learn more about the opportunities you have for finishing your degree.

2. Do your research only attend a fully accredited online College or University.

3. If ½ or more of the course offerings are online the college's commitment to online learning is strong.

4. A friend of mine received her Doctorate online as a result she increased her income and her job opportunities.

5. A decade ago few Colleges offered classes online now 100s of Colleges and Universities offer classes online.

6. Some of the advantages of online learning include the following; you can attend classes in the comfort of your own Home you can make use of special support services and tutorials and you can learn at your own pace.

7. Online learning occurs in countries around the world and 1000s of students learn in virtual classrooms every day.

8. Though class size varies many classes limit the number of participants to twenty students.

9. One of the results of online learning is improved Writing Skills good writing skills will benefit you throughout your career.

10. Finishing your education is what's important get your Degree online or attend college at a local University.

Keys to Lesson 7 Skill Builders

Key to Capitalization Skill Builder

Next year the president of my company will provide a financial incentive for all employees, and I plan to participate in it. Jack Edwards, vice president of finance, will administer the plan. Everyone in my department is looking forward to having the opportunity to save more. A pamphlet entitled, "Financial Incentives for Long-term Savings," will describe the plan and be distributed next week. If the pamphlet has not arrived by Friday, I will check with the vice president's office to find out the details.

Key to Number Skill Builder

1. We are meeting on January 5 at 10 a.m. at our offices on Lake Street.
2. Call me on Monday at 407-555-1212.
3. Alex lists his address as 407 South Maple Street, Hobart, IN 46368.
4. We received hundreds of calls about the job opening but only five resumes.
5. Purchase 12 laptops but only 7 new printers for our department.

Lesson 7 End Notes

1. William A. Sabin, *The Gregg Reference Manual*, Tenth Edition, McGraw-Hill/Irwin, 2005.
2. Dona Young, *Business English: Writing for the Global Workplace*, McGraw-Hill Higher Education, Burr Ridge, 2008, page 208.
3. Ibid., pages 212-213.

8

Quotation Marks, Apostrophes, and Hyphens

Now it is time to work on the minor marks of punctuation. While major marks such as the comma or semicolon relate to sentence structure, these minor marks relate to displaying sentence parts correctly. Nonetheless, quotation marks, apostrophes, and hyphens occur frequently: learning how to use them correctly will improve the quality of your writing.

Quotation Marks

The primary reasons for using quotation marks are as follows:[1]

1. Inserting a direct quote of three or fewer lines within the body of a document.
2. Identifying technical terms, business jargon, or coined expressions that may be unfamiliar.
3. Using words humorously or ironically.
4. Showing a slang expression, poor grammar, or an intentionally misspelled word.

However, do not use quotation marks to make a word stand out, for example:

That is a really "good" idea.

In the above example, your reader will assume that you really do not mean the idea is *good* because the reader may assume you were being sarcastic. To avoid overuse of quotation marks, follow this motto:

When in doubt, leave quotations out.

Now let's look at how to display quotation marks correctly.

Quotation Marks with Periods and Commas

One of the reasons that quotation marks confuse writers is that there are two basic ways to display them: the **closed style** and the **open style**. Here is the major difference between the two:

- **Closed style:** Place commas and periods on the inside of quotation marks.

- **Open style:** Place commas and periods on the outside of quotation marks.

Here are a few examples:

Closed:	Bill's exact words were, "That dog can't hunt."
	The president said that he wanted "the data," but which data?
Open:	Reginald described the situation as "grim but not hopeless".
	Terry instructed me to put the package in the "boot of the car", so I did.

If you live in the United States, use the closed style; if you live in Great Britain, use the open style. The style recommended in this book is the **closed style**.

Quotation Marks with Semicolons and Colons

For semicolons and colons, *always* place the quotation marks on the inside of the semicolon or colon, for example:

Senior management wants us to "go the extra mile"; however, everyone seems to be burnt out already.

Bryan said, "George's bid is overpriced": Is that correct?

According to policy, "Distribution of funds can be made only before the 15th of the month"; therefore, your funds will be sent in 10 days.

Quotation Marks with Questions and Exclamations

When using quotation marks with a question mark or an exclamation point, determine whether the question or exclamation is part of the quote or the entire sentence, for example:

Did Margarite say, "Rose is getting married next month"?

Fred asked, "How do you know?"

Margarite said, "Rose is getting married next month!"

I just won "the grand prize"!

Short Quotes and Long Quotes

Display short quotations (three lines or less) with quotation marks, leaving the quote in the body of the paragraph. However, for quotations four lines or longer, do not use quotation marks; instead set off the quote from the body of your writing by indenting it by five spaces on each side.

According to Campbell, "Protein, the most sacred of all nutrients, is a vital component of our bodies and there are hundreds of thousands of different kinds."[2] Different kinds of proteins play different roles in health and nutrition, and some of these are discussed.

Quotation within a Quotation

When you need to display a quotation within a quotation, use the single quotation mark (') for the inner quotation and the double quotation mark (") for the outer quotation, for example:

Bob said, "I'm not going to 'insult' George by inviting him to the meeting."

Note: Use the closed quotation style in the practice exercises on the following page.

Skill Builder

Quotation Marks

Instructions: Place closed quotation marks where needed in the following sentences, for example:

> **Incorrect:** Beth's exact words were, "I'll be in Boston next week".
>
> **Corrected:** Beth's exact words were, "I'll be in Boston next week."

1. My answer to your request is an enthusiastic "yes".
2. If you send the "contract", we'll sign it.
3. The code was "307A", not "370A".
4. All he wrote was, "Our dog can hunt".
5. If you call that "good timing", I don't know how to respond.

Note: See page 136 for the answer key to the above sentences.

Apostrophes

The apostrophe is used for contractions and possessives. Possessives are a bit more complicated than contractions, so let's review possessives first.

Possessives

When a noun shows possession of another noun, the apostrophe is used to show ownership. Regular nouns are made possessive as follows:

- For a singular possessive noun, place the apostrophe before the s ('s).
- For a plural possessive noun, place the apostrophe after the s (s').
- If a noun ends in an s, add an apostrophe and s ('s) or simply an apostrophe (').

Here are a few examples:

Singular Possessive	Plural Possessive
the cat's whiskers	the cats' toys
the dog's bone	the dogs' bones
Mary's books	my friends' books

Here are a few examples of names and other nouns ending in *s* showing possession:

Francis' new job *or* Francis's new job

Mr. Jones' office *or* Mr. Jones's office

When pronunciation would sound awkward with the extra syllable, do not add the *s* after the apostrophe, as follows:

Los Angeles' weather

the witnesses' replies

Irregular nouns are a bit tricky: place the apostrophe before the s ('s) for both singular and plural possession:

Singular Possessive	**Plural Possessive**
the child's coat	the children's toys
the woman's comment	the women's comments
a man's advice	the men's sporting event

The easiest way to work with plural possessives—whether regular or irregular—is to make the noun plural first and then show the possession.

To show joint possession, place the apostrophe after the second name, for example:

Janet and Bob's car

To show individual possession, place the apostrophe after each name, for example:

Janet's and Bob's cars

Next, let's look at a category of possessives that often goes unnoticed, inanimate possessives.

Inanimate Possessives

Possessives are easier to spot when a person possesses an object, such as *Bob's car*. However, an inanimate object, such as the "wind" or the "newspaper" can also show possession, for example:

> the wind's force
>
> the newspaper's headline

To know if a word shows possession, flip it around. If you need to use the word "of," in all likelihood the word shows possession, for example:

the headline of the newspaper	the newspaper's headline
the force of the wind	the wind's force
the ending of the play	the play's ending
the work of the day	the day's work
the cover of the book	the book's cover
the fender of the car	the car's fender

Now let's look at another common use of apostrophes: contractions.

Contractions

Some words, primarily verbs, are able to be shortened by omitting a few letters and using the apostrophe in their place, for example:

Verb	Contraction
will not	won't
cannot	can't
did not	didn't
should not	shouldn't

Contractions are acceptable for e-mail; however, avoid using contractions for formal or academic writing. One contraction that creates a lot of problems for writers is "it's." *It's* is the contraction for "it is" or "it has." The possessive pronoun "its" has no apostrophe.

Skill Builder

Apostrophes: Possessives and Contractions

Instructions: Make corrections where needed in the following sentences, for example:

Incorrect: Its all in a days work.

Corrected: It's all in a day's work.

1. My supervisors report wont be ready until next week.

2. The weather report says its going to rain later, but I dont believe it.

3. Though its Junes responsibility, its in Jacks best interest to complete the task.

4. Dr. Jones office isnt located down the hall; its next to Dr. Raines.

5. If you tell me its Tess project, i'll adjust my expectations.

Note: See page 136 for the answer key to the above sentences.

Hyphens

Here are some of the primary uses of hyphens:

1. To divide words.

2. To form group modifiers.

3. To display fractions and numbers above twenty-one.

4. To form certain prefixes and suffixes.

Word Division

Because computers have basically eliminated the need to divide words at the end of lines, only a brief comment about word division is included here. When dividing words, make sure you divide between syllables. If you are unsure of a word's syllabication, look it up: *When in doubt, check it out.* However, avoid dividing words whenever possible.

Compound Modifiers

Using hyphens for compound modifiers merits attention. Compound modifiers are formed when two adjectives come together to modify a noun jointly, for example:

long-term project	two-word modifiers
first-quarter report	short-term earnings
second-class service	first-class accommodations

When the modifiers follow the noun, do not use a hyphen. In fact, that is one way to check usage, for example:

meetings that are high powered	high-powered meetings
information that is up to date	up-to-date information
a woman who is well dressed	a well-dressed woman

Another way to test if you need a hyphen is to check one word at a time to see if the combination makes sense; for example, the "long-term report" is neither a "long report" nor a "term report." Both words together form one unit of meaning, which adding the hyphen accomplishes.

When two or more compound modifiers occur in sequence, use a suspension hyphen. A suspension hyphen occurs at the end of the first modifier followed by a space. Notice how the suspension hyphen is displayed below:

The short- and long-term prognoses are both excellent.

The 30- and 60-day rates are available.

Numbers

Compound numbers from twenty-one to ninety-nine are hyphenated. Here are a few examples:

thirty-three   forty-nine   seventy-three

So the next time that you write a check, make sure that you display your words correctly! Also display fractions standing alone as words, and use a hyphen, for example:

one-half   two-thirds   one-quarter

Prefixes and Suffixes

Rules about prefixes and suffixes can be complicated, so check a detailed reference manual for specific questions. Here are a few points about common uses of hyphens with prefixes or suffixes:

- Use a hyphen after the prefix *self*, for example:

  self-confidence   self-esteem

  self-addressed   self-employed

- Use a hyphen after the prefix *re* when the same spelling could be confused with another word of the same spelling but with a different meaning: [2]

  I re-sent the papers.   I resent your comment.

  He will re-sign the contract.   I will resign immediately.

  Sue will re-lease her car.   Sue will release her car.

- Use a hyphen after a prefix that is attached to a proper noun, as follows:

  ex-President Carter   trans-Atlantic flight

  pro-American policy   pre-Roman period

Work on the practice below, applying the principles you have just learned.

Skill Builder

Hyphens

Instructions: Make corrections as needed in the following sentences to show correct use of hyphens.

> **Incorrect:** The short term progress is good.
>
> **Corrected:** The short-term progress is good.

1. Your first class treatment has impressed all of us.
2. The finance department approved one half of our budget.
3. The short and long term outlooks are quite different.
4. Twenty five people attended the conference.
5. Do you have sufficient funding for your 30 and 60 day payment schedules?

Note: See page 136 for the answer key to the above sentences.

Workshop Activity

Instructions: Work with a partner to complete the Skills Workshop. After you complete Worksheets 1 and 2, you will be ready to work on Lesson 9: Similar Words and Spelling Tips.

Recap

Below is a summary how to use quotation marks, apostrophes, and hyphens.

➢ Use closed punctuation as follows:

  ▪ Place periods and commas inside of quotation marks.

  ▪ Place semicolons and colons outside of quotation marks.

  ▪ Place question marks and exclamation marks based on the meaning of the sentence.

➢ Use the apostrophe to show possession:

  ▪ With singular nouns, use an apostrophe plus *s*: *cat's meow*.

  ▪ With plural nouns, use an apostrophe after the *s*: *dogs' bones*.

  ▪ With inanimate objects, use an apostrophe, as in the *wind's force*.

  ▪ For joint ownership, place the apostrophe after the second noun: *Reggie and Grey's vacation*.

  ▪ To show individual ownership, place the apostrophe after each noun: *Janet Sue's and Dinkie's cars*.

➢ Use hyphens as follows:

  ▪ In group modifiers, such as *first-quarter report*.

  ▪ With numbers *twenty-one* through *ninety-nine*.

  ▪ For certain prefixes, such as *self-confident*.

  ▪ For words that would otherwise be confused, such as *re-sent*.

Writing Workshop

Activity A. Writing Practice

Instructions: What is listening? Write a short paper on the topic of listening, defining what effective, active, and engaged listening is and what it is not. Before you begin to write, discuss the topic with a partner. Then mind map your response, and use major topics from your mind map to create a page map. Spend about a twenty minutes composing your response, and then another five minutes proofreading and editing what you wrote.

Activity B. Journal

Instructions: What do you value most in your life? Make a list of the five things that you value, such as education, finances, family, health, and so on. Now force yourself to rank order them. Next, identify how much time and effort you are devoting to the things you value most. For example, if you value health, what are you doing (or not doing) to ensure good health. Finally, is there an incongruence or inequality in how you spend your time or money and what you value in life?

Skills Workshop

Worksheet 1. Quotations, Apostrophes, and Hyphens

Instructions: Place quotations, apostrophes, and hyphens where needed in the following sentences. Note: Use the closed punctuation style.

Incorrect: Did you say that you would go "the extra mile?"

Corrected: Did you say that you would go "the extra mile"?

1.   Margarets report is a first class example of what we need.

2.   Bob asked, "may I receive a copy of the Barker proposal"?

3.   If you can prove "that dog can hunt", well sign on to the "dotted line".

4.   A one day workshop would help our part time staff.

5.   After I rejected their "proposal", Mels response was "great".

6.   Whats next on the agenda for our mid week meeting?

7.   When I said "the games over", I was referring to Bills role.

8.   A full time position is open in our accounting department.

9.   A months worth of invoices are sitting on my desk.

10. You can use Jans office until the first floor conference room is free.

Worksheet 2. Review of Commas, Semicolons, Apostrophes, and Hyphens

Instructions: Place commas, semicolons, apostrophes, and hyphens (and anything else that is needed) in the following sentences, for example:

Incorrect: Janes answer was incomplete but no one pointed that out.

Corrected: Jane's answer was incomplete, but no one pointed that out.

1. Our brokers message got lost in the shuffle so I had to find his number on the Internet.

2. When I use the term fixin to it means that Im ready to go do something.

3. Do you have any favorite colloquial terms Sasha?

4. Call to see if their account executive is available, if not dont leave a message.

5. Lets go to the second hand shop to pick up supplies for our camping trip.

6. Mandy my new sales representative called about our "delay".

7. The short and long term projections will be available after 3 PM today.

8. Its been a long day already and one half of my work is yet to be done.

9. Enclose your check in the postage paid envelope and send it to us by Friday.

10. Sandros half baked idea was a hit at our departments meeting.

Keys to Lesson 8 Skill Builders

Key to Skill Builder for Quotation Marks

1. My answer to your request is an enthusiastic "yes."
2. If you send the "contract," we'll sign it.
3. The code was "307A," not "370A."
4. All he wrote was, "Our dog can hunt."
5. If you call that "good timing," I don't know how to respond.

Key to Skill Builder for Apostrophes: Possessives and Contractions

1. My supervisor's report won't be ready until next week.
2. The weather report says it's going to rain later, but I don't believe it.
3. Though it's June's responsibility, it's in Jack's best interest to complete the task.
4. Dr. Jones's (or Dr. Jones') office isn't located down the hall; it's to Dr. Raines' (office).
5. If you tell me it's Tess's (Tess') project, I'll adjust my expectations.

Key to Skill Builder for Hyphens

1. Your first-class treatment has impressed all of us.
2. The finance department approved one-half of our budget.
3. The short- and long-term outlooks are quite different.
4. Twenty-five people attended the conference.
5. Do you have sufficient funding for your 30- and 60-day payment schedules?

End Notes

1. Dona Young, *Business English: Writing for the Global Workplace*, McGraw-Hill Higher Education, Burr Ridge, 2008, p. 327.
2. T. Colin Campbell and Thomas M. Campbell II, *The China Study*, Bendella Books, Dallas, 2004, p. 29.
3. William A. Sabin, *The Gregg Reference Manual*, Tenth Edition, McGraw-Hill/Irwin, Burr Ridge, 2005, p. 243

9

Similar Words and
Spelling Tips

Are you ready for some surprises? In all likelihood, this lesson will reveal several words that you have been using incorrectly without any clue they were "wrong." For example, did you know that *alright* is not a Standard English spelling? Or when was the last time you *loaned* someone something or drove *thru* the car wash?

Besides using common words incorrectly or spellings that "do not really exist," the English language has many common words that confuse writers. These are the words that sound alike but are spelled differently and have different meanings, such as *its* and *it's* or *affect* and *effect*. These kinds of words are called similar words or homophones.

In addition to homophones, this lesson also includes other words that can also be confusing for any variety of reasons. Like any skill, the only way to build your vocabulary is through practice and repetition and using new words in context. It is never too late to become better at spelling. Build spelling into your daily or weekly routine, targeting ten new words at a time. Keep a list of words that you are likely to misspell.

The format of this lesson is quite different from the previous lessons in that you will start out with a short pretest. Taking a pretest will help you identify the words that give you problems, but it will also help you learn the words. Now, let's start with a short pretest.

Pretest

Instructions: In the sentences below, cross out any words that are used incorrectly, and write in the correct word above it or to the right of the sentence.

1. Will that decision effect you in a positive way?

2. The principle on my loan is due on the 1st of the month.

3. My advise is for you to get a job before you buy that new car.

4. Please ensure my manager that I will return in one-half hour.

5. Its been a challenging day, but things are getting better.

6. Their are a few issues that we need to discuss.

7. The agency gave are report a new title.

8. Pat lives further from work than I do.

9. You can have a meeting everyday, if you prefer.

10. Whose going to the ballgame?

11. I enjoy movies more then I enjoy plays.

12. Megan assured that the project would be successful

13. It's alright for you to contact the manager directly.

14. I didn't mean to infer that you were late on purpose.

15. Try and be on time for the next meeting.

Note: See page 156 for the answer key to this pretest.

Part A: Tricky Combos

This part contains some of the most common similar word combos. Write two or three sentences for each word that you are serious about mastering. With each new word that you learn, the next new word becomes a bit easier to learn, even if it does not feel that way at the moment.

adverse/averse: *Adverse* is an adjective meaning *unfavorable* or *bad*; *averse* is an adjective meaning *reluctant* or *unenthusiastic*.

> I have an *adverse* reaction to dog racing.

> Jaclyn is *averse* to working on that project.

advice/advise: *Advice* is a noun and means *recommendation*; *advise* is a verb and means *to give advice or to make a recommendation*.

> Please give me some *advice* about my paper.

> I *advise* you to trust the writing process.

affect/effect: Though each of these words can be a noun and a verb, they are primarily used as follows:

> *Affect* is a verb meaning "to influence."

> *Effect* is a noun meaning "result."

When you cannot figure out which word fits, substitute its definition:

> How will this *affect* (influence) you?

> The *effect* (result) is good.

As a noun, *affect* refers to emotions and is used primarily within the field of psychology; as a verb, *effect* means "to cause to happen" or "to bring about," for example:

> My sister was diagnosed with an *affective* (emotional) disorder.

> The new policy will *effect* (bring about) change within our organization.

When in doubt, use *affect* as a verb and *effect* as a noun.

alright/all right: The word "alright" is not considered a Standard English spelling. Use *all right*. Here is a memory trick: something is either *all right* or *all wrong*, for example:

Are you feeling *all right* about the changes?

among/between: *among* is a preposition meaning *together with* or *along with*; *between* is a preposition that means basically the same thing as *among*. Use *among* when three or more people or objects are discussed, but use *between* when only two people or objects are discussed.

Among the three of us, we have all the talent we need.

Between the two of us, you have more time than I do.

appraise/apprise: *Appraise* is a verb meaning *to assess* or *evaluate*; *apprise* is a verb meaning *to inform*.

After the realtor *appraises* the house, she'll *apprise* you of your options.

are/hour/our: *Are* is a present tense form of the verb *to be*; *hour* is a noun that refers to 60 minutes of time; and *our* is the possessive pronoun for *we*.

What *are our* options? We have an *hour* to decide.

assure/ensure/insure: These three verbs are somewhat similar in sound and meaning, but they have distinct uses, for example:

Assure means "to give *someone* confidence."

Ensure means "to make certain" that some *thing* will happen.

Insure means "to protect against loss."

Here is the rule of thumb to follow: when you use *assure*, make sure that a "person" is the object, for example:

I *assure* **you** that we will meet the deadline.

When you use *ensure*, make sure that a "thing" is the object:

I *ensure* the **product** will arrive on time.

When you use *insure*, make sure that it refers to "insurance."

You can *insure* against losses with our company.

breath/breathe: breath is a noun meaning a "lungful of air"; breathe is a verb meaning "to take in breaths."

I need a *breath* of fresh air.

When I *breathe* fresh air, I feel much better.

don't/doesn't: *Don't* and *doesn't* are both contractions of *(to) do not*. *Doesn't* is the contraction of *does not*, which is the third person –s form of Editing English. However, speakers often mistakenly use *don't* for third person singular subjects when they should be using *doesn't*.

She *doesn't* have a care in the world.

Not: She *don't* have a care in the world.

Bob *doesn't* go to school here anymore

Not: Bob *don't* go to school here no more.

everyday/every day: Use *everyday* as a modifier meaning "ordinary" or "daily"; if you can insert the word "single" between *every* and *day*, you know that it is two words.

That is an *everyday* routine.

We do that procedure *every (single) day*.

farther/further: Though similar in meaning, *farther* refers to actual distance that can be measured; *further* indicates progress that is intangible and not measurable, such as "to a greater or lesser degree or extent."

She lives *farther* from work than you do.

Let's discuss this proposal *further*.

has/have: *Has* and *have* are both present tense forms of *to have*. Use *has* for third person singular (he *has*, she *has*, and it *has*) and *have* for all other persons: I *have*, you *have*, we *have* and they *have*. However, writers sometimes use *have* for third person singular in place of *has*.

A block of rooms *has* been reserved.

Not: A block (of rooms) *have* been reserved.

The car *has* a few dents on its fender.

Not: The car *have* a few dents on its fender.

infer/imply: These two verbs are opposite in meaning: *infer* means "to deduce, conclude, or assume"; *imply* means "to express or state indirectly."

From your statement, I *inferred* that Len was at the meeting; is that what you meant to *imply*?

its/it's: The word *its* is a possessive pronoun, whereas *it's* is a contraction of *it is* or *it has*, for example:

You can't judge a book by *its* cover.

It's been a great day.

Writing Tip
One way to improve your use of these words is to stop using the contraction for *it is* and *it has*; in addition, every time you use *it's*, check the spelling by substituting "it is."

loan/lend: Most people confuse these words without realizing it, even people in high level banking positions! Here is what you need to know:

Loan is a *noun*, not an action.

Lend is a *verb*; its past tense form is "lent."

The bank will give you a *loan*, but it will *lend* you money.

In other words, you cannot really "loan" someone your book, but you can "lend" it. Practice these words a few times, and their meanings will make more sense each time you use them correctly.

may be/maybe: *May be* is a verb form that suggests possibility; *maybe* is an adverb that means "perhaps."

This week *may be* the right time to submit our request.

Maybe you can get the information from Fred.

principal/principle: At one point, you may have learned that the *principal* of your school was your "pal." That is true; however, *principal* has a broader meaning, which is "chief or main." So you may be surprised to learn that your loan consists of "*principal* and interest." *Principle* means "theory or rule of conduct."

What is the *principal* on your loan?

We all try to live by our *principles*.

In fact, I would rather pay my *principal* than my interest!

saw/seen: *Saw* is the past tense of the verb *to see*; *seen* is the past participle. The past tense form of a verb does not take a helper verb; however, the past participle form must have a helper. Contrary to Edited American English usage, speakers sometimes use a helper with *saw* but leave out the helper with *seen*.

We all *saw* Tasha enter the conference room.

Not: We all *seen* Tasha enter the conference room.

We had *seen* that movie twice already.

Not: We had *saw* that movie twice already.

sight/site/cite: *Sight* is a noun referring to vision or mental perception; *site* is also a noun that refers to a location, as in Web site; *cite* is a verb meaning *to quote* or *to name*.

The pilot's *sight* was impaired due to the accident.

My Web *site* is under construction.

I was *cited* for driving without my license.

supposed to/used to: In speech the –ed ending of *supposed* and *used* is not always distinguished from the –t of *to*. Therefore, in writing, the –ed is often erroneously left off of these words. Remember that these words are regular verbs and as such require the –ed ending for their past tense and past participle forms.

You *are supposed* to attend that class. I *used* to go to that school.

Not: You are *suppose* to assist in the lab.

than/then: the word *than* is a conjunction used in comparisons; *then* is an adverb referring to time, as in "after that." To help remember, use *then* when it has to do with a "*when.*"

I would rather get up early *than* sleep late.

After you complete the project, *then* I will have more time.

their/there/they're: *Their* is the possessive form of *they* and will always be followed by a noun; *there* is an adverb meaning "in or at *that* place" or a pronoun which functions as an anticipating subject; *they're* is the contracted form of *they are*

Their apartment is next to mine.

There are a lot of people in the lobby. Go *there* if you choose.

They're standing next to the reception desk.

themselves/theirselves: *Themselves* is the reflexive form of *they*; *theirselves* is not a Standard English spelling.

The team members can help *themselves* to refreshments.

through/threw/thorough/thru: *Through* is a preposition meaning *by means of, from beginning to end,* or *because of; threw* is a verb and the past participle of *throw; thorough* is an adjective meaning *carried through to completion;* and take special note: *thru* is a "word" that does not exist in Standard English—use *thru* only as a part of the term "drive-thru."

Walk *through* the room quietly.

Jenkins *threw* the paper at the judge.

We all did a *thorough* job on the report.

to/too: The preposition *to* is often used when the adverb *too* should be used. Remember, when you are describing something that relates to quantity, use the adverb *too.* Also use *too* when you could substitute the word *also.*

It's *too* late to go to the meeting.

The proposal has *too* much fluff and *too* little substance besides being *too* late to make a difference.

I will go to the conference *too* (also).

try to/"try and": The verb *try* is not followed by the word "and." Instead, *try* is followed by an infinitive, such "to be," "to see," "to go," and so on. Many people inadvertently say "*Try and* be on time" when they really mean to say "*Try to be* on time."

Try to get your work done early.

Try to be there before anyone else.

were/we're/where/wear: *Were* is one of the past-tense forms of the verb *to be* (as in *you were, we were, they were*). *We're* is a contraction for *we are*. The adverb *where* (pronounced the same as *wear*) is often confused with the past tense verb *were*. The verb *wear* means *to dress in*.

Where were you when the decision was made?

We're about to enter a new phase.

Wear that suit to the meeting.

who's/whose: The contraction *who's* stands for *who is* or *who has*. *Whose* is the possessive pronoun of *who*.

Who's chairing the meeting?

Whose book is that?

you/yous/y'all: *You* is a subjective pronoun, and *you* is singular or plural. In some areas, such as Chicago, the word *yous* is used as a local language plural form of *you*, as in *yous guys*. While this is considered colloquial in the United States, *yous* is an acceptable pronoun in Ireland.

You all should go to the game this Friday.

In Southern portions of the U.S., the equivalent to *yous* is *y'all*, with *all y'all* being used with larger groups. An additional form is *you'uns* or *you'ins*. These variations add life and color to the language when speaking; however, edit them to standard usage in your writing so that people from all parts of the globe can understand the meaning of your message.

you're/your: *You're* is a contraction for *you are*. *Your* is a possessive pronoun for *you*.

You're the one I want on my team.

Your personality makes the difference.

The above list of similar words along with those that appear in *A Quick Guide to Similar Words* (located at the end of this book) are only a handful of the similar words that you will come across. By doing the Workshop Activity below, you will see how extensive the list of similar words actually is.

Workshop Activity

Instructions: Go to the Internet to research similar words, homophones, or homonyms. Make your own list of troublesome words.

Part B. Spelling Tips

One of the reasons spelling is difficult is that only about 40 percent of English words are spelled according to phonetics, which means "spelled the way they sound." In other words, about 60 percent of English words are written with silent letters or other non-phonetic qualities, thereby requiring them to be memorized.

Here are some suggestions that you can use to improve your spelling and vocabulary usage:

- **Make a running list of words that you find challenging.**

  The way you use language is unique. Your reading, writing, and spelling skills have different strengths and weaknesses from everyone else. The way to become stronger is to tailor your studies to learning the specific words that you have a challenge with "right now." As you read, circle the words that you do not understand. Take the time to look them up.

- **Use new words in context: write two or three sentences with each new word.**

  Unless you practice a new word in context, your work is not very meaningful. By writing two or three sentences, you are applying the new word in a way that will make it easier to remember and use correctly.

- **As you learn a new word, check the correct pronunciation..**

  Break up the new word into syllables and use the dictionary guidelines for pronunciation. Ask a friend to pronounce the word for you; say the word out loud several times until you own it.

- **Use spelling rules that are easy to remember.**

  Though most spelling rules will not aid you, a few will. For example, the rule "use *i* before *e* except after *c* or when the sound is like *a* as in *neighbor*" is easy to remember and helpful. However, learning complex spelling rules that have a lot of exceptions may not be as helpful. Go to the Internet and Google "spelling rules." Glean what you need, and then move on.

- **Learn some of the Latin and Greek roots of words as well as prefixes and suffixes.**

  Learning roots, prefixes, and suffixes will help you figure out new words and gain a deeper understanding of the words you already know. A few are listed below.

A Sampling of Roots, Prefixes, and Suffixes

Root	Meaning	Origin
anthrop	man	Greek
biblio	book	Greek
cent	one hundred	Latin
equ	equal, fair	Latin
geo	earth	Greek
hydro	water	Greek
ortho	straight	Greek
psych	mind, soul, spirit	Greek
sci	to know	Latin
techn	art, skill	Greek
viv, vit	life	Latin

Prefix	Meaning	Example
a- or an-	not, without	amoral, apolitical
ab-	away from	abduction
ambi-	both	ambidextrous
anti-	against	antisocial
bene-	good	beneficial
contra	against	contradict
dis	not part of	disengage
ex	out from	exhale
hyper	over	hypertension, hyperactive
il, im, in	not	illegal, impossible, indivisible
inter	between	interstate
ir	not	irreversible
macro	large	macrocosm
micro	small	microcosm
mis	wrong	misconduct
mono	one	monologue
post	after	postpone
pre	before	pretest
pseudo	false	pseudonym
re	do again	repeat
semi	half	semiannual
sub	under	subversive
trans	across	transport

Suffix	Meaning	Example
age	result of action	courage
cide	kill	homicide
ectomy	cutting	appendectomy

ful	amount that fills	handful
ic, tic, ical	having to do with	dramatic, Biblical
ism	the belief in	mysticism
logy	the study of	psychology, biology
ness	quality	kindness
phobia	fear	claustrophobia
ship	condition, status	ownership

Workshop Activity

Instructions:

1. Select five Greek or Latin roots. For each root, identify two words that were developed from it.
2. Go to the Internet and search for a more complete list of roots, prefixes, and suffixes. Use your lists to develop a study plan to improve your vocabulary.

Recap

Improving your vocabulary will improve your critical thinking skills as well as your writing skills. Make the effort to practice new words in context: write two or threes sentences with new word and you will begin to use it with confidence.

Writing Workshop

Activity A. Writing Practice

Instructions: In the Skills Workshop, you will find 5 lists of spelling words that were taken from the 100 most commonly misspelled words. Work through each list (one list per week). Memorize the spelling for each word, and write two sentences for each word to ensure that you use it in context. Also, refer to *A Quick Reference to Similar Words*, located at the end of this book. Identify two or three sets of words that you will learn along with each spelling list. Good luck!

Activity B. Journal

Instructions: Write an honest self-assessment of your skills: Have your skills improved? What areas do you still need to work on? Do you feel more confident? Are you able to identify your mistakes and correct them? Are you committed to working on areas that still challenge you?

Skills Workshop

Worksheet 1. Similar Words

Instructions: Underline the word in parentheses that best completes the sentence

1. They have (to, too) many new projects and (to, too) little time.

2. You will be (appraised, apprised) of the situation before noon today.

3. Jackson (assured, ensured) me that you got the job.

4. If you feel (alright, all right) about it, ask for a raise.

5. (Your, you're) the right person to turn the situation around.

6. (Among, Between) the three of us, we have all the resources we need.

7. Try (and, to) see Leonard before you leave today.

8. Kevin said that he would (loan, lend) me his notes.

9. His remark was a real (complement, compliment).

10. I live (farther, further) from work (than, then) you do.

11. If you (could of, could have) spoken to Della, you'd understand.

12. Vera (past, passed) that trait on to her daughters (to, too).

13. How will that (affect, effect) you?

14. When you know the (affect, effect), let me know.

15. Carol (loaned, lent) me everything I needed for the trip.

16. The project lost (its, it's) appeal after Mike quit.

17. I (ensure, assure) all print materials will be of high quality.

18. After you (ensure, assure) me, (assure, ensure) the others also.

19. (There, They're, Their) boat has left the dock.

20. We are (farther, further) along (than, then) we realize.

21. Say (its, it's) time to go, and we will.

22. If the bank will (loan, lend) you enough funds, will you buy the car?

23. My (principle, principal) and interest are due on the 1st of the month.

23. That company does all training on (sight, site).

24. Did the officer (site, cite) you for the violation?

25. We all try to live by our (principals, principles).

Worksheet 2. Similar Words

Instructions: Use each of the following words in a sentence.

1. its

_____

2. their

_____

3. than

_____

4. adverse

_____

_____

5. too

_____

6. assure

_____

7. it's

_____

8. effect

_____

9. loan

_____

10. further

_____

11. they're

_____

12. ensure

_____

13. affect

_____

14. then

_____

15. all right

_____
_____

16. doesn't

_____

17. don't

_____

18. saw

_____

19. seen

_____

20. principle

_____

Spelling Lists 1 - 5

Here are 5 lists of words: each list contains 10 of the 100 most commonly misspelled words. The best way to master these words is to use them in sentences.

Spelling List 1

1. acceptable   adj: satisfactory
2. believe   v: consider, accept as true
3. calendar   n: agenda, schedule
4. definitely   adv: absolutely, without doubt
5. existence   n: survival, subsistence, life
6. leisure   n: free time, relaxation
7. maintenance   n: preservation, looking after
8. neighbor   n: fellow citizen
9. privilege   n: honor, opportunity
10. separate   v: divide, break away; adj: unconnected, distinct

Spelling List 2

1. amateur   n: layperson, not professional
2. embarrass   v: humiliate, make self-conscious
3. conscience   n: sense of right and wrong
4. conscious   adj: aware, mindful, awake, deliberate
5. foreign   adj: overseas, unfamiliar, unrelated
6. inoculate   v: immunize, vaccinate
7. miniscule   adj: very small, tiny
8. precede   v: to go before, to lead
9. proceed   v: to go on, to carry on, to continue
10. relevant   adj: pertinent, applicable, important

Spelling List 3

1. accommodate   v: to house, to have capacity for
2. conscientious   adj: reliable, diligent, thorough
3. equipment   n: gear, tools, paraphernalia
4. hierarchy   n: rank order of things or people
5. jewelry   n: adornments
6. mischievous   adj: ill-behaved, bad, harmful
7. medieval   adj: pertaining to the Middle Ages
8. noticeable   adj: visible, evident, in plain sight
9. possession   n: ownership
10. questionnaire   n: survey, opinion poll, feedback form

Spelling List 4

1. acquire   v: to obtain, to attain
2. experience   n: knowledge, skill, familiarity; v: feel, live through
3. gauge   v: measure, estimate, judge
4. immediate   adj: urgent, high priority, instant
5. knowledge   n: information, expertise, skill, familiarity
6. license   n: authorization, permit, certificate
7. millennium   n: a thousand years
8. misspell   v: to spell incorrectly
9. occurrence   n: incident, happening, event
10. reference   n: mention, citation, note; v: to mention, to cite

Spelling List 5

1. argument   n: quarrel, disagreement
2. discipline   n: self-control, strictness, branch of learning
3. humorous   adj: funny, amusing, witty
4. ignorance   n: lack of knowledge, unawareness
5. intelligence   n: cleverness, aptitude, astuteness
6. kernel   n: core, essential part, seed
7. perseverance   n: insistence, resolve, determination
8. referred   v: recommended
9. schedule   n: agenda, timetable, plan
10. weird   adj: unusual, peculiar

Key to Lesson 9 Pretest

1. Will that decision ~~effect~~ **affect** you in a positive way?
2. The ~~principle~~ **principal** on my loan is due on the 1st of each month.
3. My ~~advise~~ **advice** is for you to get a job before you buy that new car.
4. Please ~~ensure~~ **assure** my manager that I will return in one-half hour.
5. ~~Its~~ **It's** been a challenging day, but things are getting better.
6. ~~Their~~ **There** are a few issues that we need to discuss.
7. The agency gave ~~are~~ **our** report a new title.
8. Pat lives ~~further~~ **farther** from work than I do.
9. You can have a meeting ~~everyday~~ **every day**, if you prefer.
10. ~~Whose~~ **Who's** going to the ballgame?
11. I enjoy movies more ~~then~~ **than** I enjoy plays.
12. Megan ~~assured~~ **ensured** that the project would be successful.
13. It's ~~alright~~ **all right** for you to contact the manager directly.
14. I didn't mean to ~~infer~~ **imply** that you were late on purpose.
15. Try ~~and~~ **to** be on time for the next meeting.

Lesson 9 End Notes

The following Web sites were referenced:

1. http://www.cooper.com/alan/homonym_list.html, accessed on February 4, 2008.

2. Ten Tips for Better Spelling, http://www.factmonster.com/ipka/A0903395.html, accessed on February 6, 2008.

3. Spelling It Right, http://www.spelling.hemscott.net/#advice, accessed on February 6, 2008.

4. AskOxford, Commonly Confused Words, http://www.askoxford.com/betterwriting/classicerrors/confused/?view=uk, accessed on February 8, 2008.

5. http://www.betterendings.org/homeschool/Words/Root%20Words.htm, accessed on February 8, 2008.

10

Editing Tips and Proofreading Practice

The principles you have learned so far have prepared you to proofread correctly. However, to bring your writing to its highest level of quality, you also need to develop editing skills.

- **Proofreading** is correcting errors in punctuation and grammar, making writing correct and therefore professional.

- **Editing** is changing the structure and wording of writing, making writing reader friendly.

Proofreading is your first line of defense. Decisions are based on clear criteria: you are not *changing* a document, you are *correcting* errors. Now that you have built strong proofreading skills, it is time to take some of the mystery out of editing skills. The first part of this lesson covers some principles of editing that are covered in detail in *Which Comes First, the Comma or the Pause? A Practical Guide to Writing.*

The second part of this lesson gives you additional practice applying what you have learned to real-world documents, bringing them to professional standards of accuracy.

Finally, at the end of this lesson, you will find a post-assessment. After you take the post-assessment, score your test and then compare your results with the pre-assessment that you took in Lesson 1. You will find detailed instructions at the end of this lesson. Now, go have some fun with these editing tips and proofreading exercises!

QUICK EDITING TIPS

Simple, clear, and concise writing is reader-friendly writing. But how do you achieve it? You have already started by learning about the sentence core—the sentence core is the foundation for important editing principles, such as the active voice.

The following gives you an entrée to the kinds of principles covered in serious detail in *Which Comes First the Comma or the Pause? A Practical Guide to Writing*. Applying these principles to your writing is an important step in developing an effective writing style.

Contain Sentence Length

One of the best ways to control your writing *and* help your readers understand your message is to limit sentences to 25 words or fewer.

> Sentences that are much longer than 25 words have a tendency to confuse readers because by the time that they get to the end of a long sentence, many readers have already forgotten what the beginning of the sentence was about and need to go back to the beginning and reread it again, which can be very tedious. (57 words) What do you think?

When you find yourself writing sentences that are complicated or seem longer than usual, count the number of words. If the sentence is longer than 25 words, cut words or break the information into shorter sentences—at times, you will need to do both.

Control Sentence Structure

You have already learned the importance of the sentence core. Keep the sentence core—the subject and verb—close to the beginning of the sentence. Also, put as few words or phrases as possible between your subject and verb.

The closer the subject of the sentence is to the verb, the easier it is for the reader to understand. In fact, with English, a reader or listener needs to hear both the subject *and* verb before understanding even begins.

Weak:	Carol Harris, a good friend of mine who lives in a nearby town called Mt. Vernon, will arrange the reception.
Revised:	Carol Harris will arrange the reception. By the way, she's a friend of mine who lives in Mt. Vernon, a nearby town.

As you can see, the more words you put between the subject and the verb, the more difficult the sentence is to understand.

Use Real Subjects with Strong Verbs

Real subjects drive the action of verbs; however, a *real subject* is not always the *grammatical subject* of the sentence. When the real subject and the grammatical subject are one and the same, sentences are more powerfully written. You have already learned how to identify the grammatical subject, which precedes the verb in a statement. Now let's work with the following sentence to identify the *real subject*:

The meeting was chaired by Mike.

In the above example, the verb is "was chaired" and the grammatical subject is "meeting." However, "meeting" does not perform the action of the verb. To find the real subject, ask *"who" chaired the meeting?* Your answer is "Mike." Now move "Mike" to the grammatical subject position (preceding the verb), making the real subject also the grammatical subject:

Mike chaired the meeting.

One way to test the strength of your writing is to check the strength of your verbs. When you can, avoid weak verbs, such as *is, make, give,* and *take.* Starting sentences with *it is* or *there are* is also a clue that your sentence may be getting off to a weak start. Though you cannot edit out all of your "it is" sentences, edit out as many as you can.

Weak	It is an interesting plot.
Revised	The plot holds the reader's interest.

Weak	There are issues to discuss.
Revised	We need to discuss some issues.

Real subjects and strong verbs also relate to using the active voice, which is briefly reviewed below.

Write in the Active Voice

The active voice is one of the most important qualities of effective writing. To understand active voice, let's start with a passive sentence:

Passive: The papers were sent to Sue by Bob.

First, identify the main verb, which is *sent*. Next, identify the real subject, which is the person or thing that performed the action of the verb. So ask yourself, *who sent the papers? Bob did.*

Active: Bob sent the papers to Sue.

Here are the steps to change a sentence from passive to active voice:

1.   Identify the main verb of the sentence.
2.   Identify the real subject by asking, *who performed the action of the verb?*
3.   Place the real subject at the beginning of the sentence.
4.   Follow the real subject with the verb, making adjustments for agreement.
5.   Complete the sentence with the rest of the information.

Let's use the above "formula" to translate another sentence from passive to active voice:

Passive: The merger was rejected by their new CEO.

1. What is the main verb?   Rejected

2. Who was doing the rejecting?	their new CEO
3. Begin the sentence with the real subject:	Their new CEO . . .
4. Follow the real subject with the verb:	Their new CEO rejected . . .
5. Complete the sentence:	Their new CEO rejected the merger.

Here is the structure for the **passive voice**: *What was done by whom and why.*

Here is the structure for the **active voice**: *Who did what and why.*

Can you see that by changing from the passive to the active voice, your writing becomes more direct, clear, and concise?

Be Concise

With writing, *less is more*. Therefore, present your message in the most concise fashion possible. Cutting words is one of the first editing tasks you should work on. Why edit or revise sentences only to cut them later?

When you compose, do not waste your energy trying to be concise—you are likely to lose your train of thought. After your ideas are developed, cut redundant information and excess words.

| **Wordy:** | I am writing to let you know that your order is ready. |
| **Concise:** | Your order is ready. |

| **Wordy:** | When you write down your words on any subject, try to be concise in the way that you use words to get across the meaning that you are trying to convey. |
| **Concise:** | When you write, be concise. |

Adjust Your Tone

Tone relates to how you state your message. Whenever possible, state your message in a positive and affirmative way. Focusing on your reader rather than yourself also improves the tone of your message: use the *you* viewpoint rather than the *I* viewpoint when feasible.

Positive means constructive: state what will go well if conditions are met rather than what will *not* go well if conditions are *not* met.

Negative: If you do not return your purchase within 10 days, we cannot help you.

Positive: If you return your purchase within 10 days, we can help you.

Negative: If you do not ask the right question, you will not get the right answer.

Positive: If you ask the right question, you will get the right answer.

The following examples shift from the *you* viewpoint to the *I* viewpoint:

***I* Viewpoint:** *I* would like to ask if you could attend our department meeting.

***You* Viewpoint:** Could *you* attend our department meeting?

***I* Viewpoint:** *I* have not received your application.

***You* Viewpoint:** *Your* application has not arrived.

Manage Information Flow

Managing information flow aids readers in understanding your message. To manage information flow, you first need to identify which aspects of your topic are familiar to your reader and which are unfamiliar. Familiar information is considered "old information." Unfamiliar information is considered "new information."

Put familiar information at the beginning of your sentence and unfamiliar information toward the end. The familiar information helps anchor your reader so that the new information is easier to comprehend.

***New* to Old:** *How to plan retirement on a fixed income* was reviewed in the seminar.

Old to *New*: The seminar reviewed *how to plan retirement on a fixed income*.

In the above sentences, "the seminar" is considered old information because the reader is more familiar with that topic. "How to plan retirement on a fixed income" extends the reader's knowledge of the topic, so it is considered new information. Here is another example:

New to Old: *The man across the room in the grey suit* is the person you are looking for.

Old to New: The person you are looking for is *the man across the room in the grey suit.*

For balance, all sentences should have a mix of old and new information. Any sentence that contains all old information is redundant and should be cut or revised. Any sentence that contains all new information should be revised because it will seem disconnected from the rest of the information.

Modify Sparingly but Correctly

Unless you are writing a novel, use modifiers sparingly. Words such as "very" and "really" tend to take away from your meaning rather than add to it. Here is a rule of thumb for using modifiers: *When in doubt, take the modifier out.*

Your comment was *very* interesting.   Your comment was interesting.

Joe was *really* late to the meeting.   Joe was late to the meeting.

Keep a modifying word or phrase close to the word it is modifying.

Misplaced Modifier: The *stapler* was on the table *that Jill bought*.
Corrected: The *stapler that Jill bought* was on the table.

Misplaced Modifier: *Walking into the room*, Alice's coffee spilled.
Corrected: *Walking into the room, Alice* spilled her coffee.

Misplaced Modifier: An *airplane* cruised onto the runway *with a burning engine*.
Corrected: An *airplane with a burning engine* cruised onto the runway.

Be on the alert for misplaced modifiers—readers can pick them out easier than the person writing them. In fact, you will find that many misplaced modifiers are funny when you stop to analyze what the sentence actually means.

Use Simple Words

Using simple words keeps your writing reader friendly. In fact, a good rule of thumb is to write the way you would speak: *If you would not say it that way, do not write it that way.* This advice applies especially to verbs, such as the following:

Complicated	**Simplified**
We *endeavor* to meet client needs.	We *try* to meet client needs.
Our company *utilizes* that vendor.	Our company *uses* that vendor.
We are *terminating* that program.	We are *ending* that program.
Marvin *contemplates* that we will gain additional revenue.	Marvin *thinks* that we will gain additional revenue.

What other words have you noticed people using that sound too formal?

Avoid Outdated Expressions and Clichés

Some outdated expressions seem to stay in constant use, having been recycled since before the 1950s:

Outdated Expressions	**Current Use**
per your request	as you requested
per our conversation	as we discussed
attached please find	attached is …
thank you in advance	thank you

Take *per* out of your vocabulary unless you are using it as "by," as in "price *per* pound."

Avoid Split Infinitives

As you will remember, an infinitive is "to" plus the base form or a verb, such as "to go." Splitting an infinitive is not actually incorrect, but a split infinitive is a structure to avoid, when possible. Therefore, if a split infinitive does not clearly improve the quality of a sentence, do not split the infinitive.

How would you revise, "To boldly go where no man has gone"? Which version do you prefer, your revision or the original?

Let's move from editing tips to proofreading exercises.

APPLYING PROOFREADING SKILLS

This section includes several e-mail messages that contain errors. Correct the errors in punctuation, capitalization, number usage, word usage, and anything else you find. The key to these exercises is located at the end of this lesson following the posttest.

Practice Exercise A

Dear Manager,

On July 21st, 2004 i purchased four tires at your Shop in Chesterton IN.

After I bought the tires my car began to shake and i was concered. When I had the vehicle checked i was told that the car was out of Alignment. That is the reason why i needed to bye new tires to begin with. You insured me that you would fix this problem.

Please let me know how you plan to remedy this problem i need my car fixed and have already invested my time energy and money.

sincerely,

Dama

Practice Exercise B

Hi Sasha,

Account #2345 needs a credit of 250 dollars. Originally a deposit for 125.00 was made on 2/24 but on 2.25 the Customer received a Debit rather than a credit. The customer, hasnt been credited yet even though we ensured her that her Account would be brought up to date by 2-28.

If YOU can get back to me on this issue ASAP i would appreciate it.

Best Regards,

Silva

Practice Exercise C

Good morning,

I just wanted to say Thank You for allowing me to change my work schedle it means so much to me too finally be able to work with Manaagement, who understand not only the employer needs but the employe needs as well.

Thank You again.

Jeff

Practice Exercise D

Michelle,

I am wonder if you have writen a piece, or have information on which Market sectors look positive going forward in 2008? In addition i am looking for information on which sectors do not look favorabile in 2008?

Do you know where i can find this information?

Thank You in advance.

Pat

Practice Exercise E

Hey Mitch

How ru today??? i spoke w/Deb about the prob. We r havng w/ r software and she said its something ur working on but i want to be sure b4 i lv for the day.

Im pretty sure that i will be hear early in the AM tom so give me a call tom if you cant reach me tonite. If we cn have it fix by fri than we will be set for the wkend.

Are you ok w/that?

DJ

Practice Exercise F

Geo,

I have reviewed the Quote and everything looks alright, ill sign the quote and fax it back today, if you need any thing else signed please bring it on fri and we can take care of it in the meeting. By the way did u know that we r having another mtg on wed feb 21? Thx.

Thom

Practice Exercise G

Thom,

Attached please find the quote for the Cabling Project in the Kennedy Bldg. I see u on mon at the mtg. if you need any thing from me before than let me know. Weve been experiencing some problems w/ r photocopier so the copy may not be to clear. Call me if u cant read it.

Geo

Practice Exercise H

Ralph,

The Architects and i have put a schedule together showing the various tasks that need to be accomplished and when so we will be ready to start construction when the rest of the blueprints are turned over to us which should happen by the end of next week or so and i assume thats alright with you.

Call me if you want more info on this project ill be hear most of the rest of the day.

Marge

Recap

You have just completed intensive work to improve your writing skills, and you should be making writing decisions faster and with more confidence. If not, identify what is holding you back and do more work in that area.

Writing is the key to a successful career in today's world. On just about every job, you will find yourself writing e-mail messages on a daily basis. Other than e-mail, you will be writing proposals and evaluations of yourself and those you manage. Any efforts you put forth to improve your writing skills will pay off in big dividends in the years to come. *Buona fortuna!*

Writing Workshop

Activity A. Writing Practice

Instructions: Write a short- and long-range plan. What are your goals six months from now? What do you want to achieve five years from now? What other goals do you have? What books could you read to help you achieve your dreams? What daily activities can you plan in your routine to help you achieve what you want in life?

For example, do you need to learn more about managing your finances? There is a saying, "It's not how much you earn but how you manage what you earn." What does that mean to you? What changes can you make now to ensure that you have a more secure future?

Activity B. Journal

Instructions: Write an honest self-assessment of how your skills have improved. Compare your pre- and post-assessments. What areas do you still need to work on? Are you able to identify your mistakes and correct them? Are you committed to working on areas that still challenge you? Do you feel more confident?

After you have worked on the Writing Workshop exercises, write yourself a letter of recommendation identifying your best qualities and highlighting your skills and abilities. Though you will not be able to use it as a reference for a job, you can use it to remind yourself of your accomplishments and how far you have come.

Skills Workshop

Post-Assessment

Complete the following assessment so that you can accurately gauge your current skills. After you take this post-assessment, score it. The answers are in the back of the book in **Keys to Assessments and Worksheets**. Compare your results with your pre-assessment, using the score sheet that follows the key to the post-assessment.

It's not about the test: It's about what you learn. Few people are able to achieve a perfect score, so try to let go of feelings of disappointment if your post-assessment is not perfect. Instead, use your test results to identify what you need to learn next.

Part A. Punctuation: Commas and Semicolons

Instructions: Place commas and semicolons where needed in the following sentences.

1. When Jason presents his information assist him with the handouts.

2. Plan to attend the meeting on Wednesday April 15 at 9 o'clock.

3. Chicago Illinois is the location we have chosen for our conference.

4. I will make the arrangements for our retreat however Miller will help.

5. When things don't go as you planned keep an open mind.

6. Everyone would like to get the promotion but it can only go to one person.

7. You will do well in Phoenix you prepared for everything that could go wrong.

8. However you should still remain humble until it is over.

9. David you have been a great support the last few weeks.

10. You can bring a guest with you to the dinner if you wish.

11. Although Bob helped me on the assignment I did not do well enough to pass.

12. My professor however said that I could repeat it.

13. The opportunity will not present itself again do your best.

14. You can accept their offer you will not regret it.

15. Mitchell my cousin will be here for lunch today.

Part B. Capitalization, Quotation Marks, and Apostrophes

Instructions: Make corrections in capitalization, apostrophes, and quotation marks as well as any other errors you may find.

The Restaurant that i interviewed with finally got back to me. The job that i was applying for was a Managers position. For the past week or so, i have been concerned about some of my answer's and missing information on my resume. Then I sent the Assistant Manager a note asking him, "would you like for me to send you an updated resume"? Since I had not heard back from him, i assumed it was because i didn't do well. Every time I felt bad, I said to myself, "don't worry—you gave it your best—no one is perfect". Would you believe it if I told you they offered me the job? Of course, I will accept it—a managers position is exactly what I was hoping to find.

Part C. Similar Words

Instructions: Correct word usage in the following sentences.

11. How much do you pay in principle and interest?

12. The affect of the problem was not yet known.

13. Can you ensure me that the assignment will be in on time?

14. Bob's decision to hire a new employee will effect my job.

15. If you will loan me your car, I will take good care of it.

16. My car loses it's traction on icy roads.

17. When you say they're reports are late, do you mean all reports?

18. If you say its time to renew our membership, we will.

19. Adams asked if their are issues that we need to resolve.

20. Live by your principals, and you will have fewer regrets.

Part D. Number Usage

Instructions: Correct number usage in the following sentences.

1. Alice brought 10 notebooks, but we needed only 5.

2. The meeting was held on November 12th last year.

3. Do you live at 1200 W. Jarwin?

4. Alyssa has 100s of friends.

5. The contract was worth one point five million dollars.

Keys to Lesson 10 Practice Exercises

Key to Practice Exercise A

Dear Manager,

On July 21, 2004, I purchased four tires at your shop in Chesterton, Indiana. After I bought the tires, my car began to shake and I was concerned. When I had the vehicle checked, I was told that the car was out of alignment. That is the reason why I needed to buy new tires to begin with. You assured me that you would fix this problem.

Please let me know how you plan to remedy this problem. I need my car fixed and have already invested my time, energy, and money.

Sincerely,

Dama

Key to Practice Exercise B

Hi Sasha,

Account No. 2345 needs a credit of $250. Originally, a deposit for $125 was made on February 24, but on February 25, the customer received a debit rather than a credit.

The customer hasn't been credited yet, even though we assured her that her account would be brought up to date by February 28.

If you can get back to me on this issue ASAP, I would appreciate it.

Best regards,

Silva

Key to Practice Exercise C

Good morning,

I just wanted to say thank you for allowing me to change my work schedule. It means so much to me to work with management who understand not only the employer's needs but the employee's needs as well.

Jeff

Key to Practice Exercise D

Michelle,

I am wondering if you have written a piece or have information on which market sectors look positive going forward in 2008. In addition, I am looking for information on which sectors do not look favorable in 2008.

Do you know where I can find this information?

Thank you.

Pat

Key to Practice Exercise E

Hi Mitch,

How are you today? I spoke with Deb about the problem we are having with our software; and she said it's something you are working on, but I want to be sure before I leave for the day.

I'm pretty sure that I will be here early in the morning tomorrow, so give me a call tomorrow if you can't reach me tonight. If we can have it fixed by Friday, then we will be set for the weekend.

Are you OK with that?

DJ

Key to Practice Exercise F

Geo,

I have reviewed the quote, and everything looks all right. I'll sign the quote and fax it back today. If you need anything else signed, please bring it on Friday; we can take care of it in the meeting.

By the way, did you know that we are having another meeting on Wednesday, February 21?

Thanks.

Thom

Key to Practice Exercise G

Thom,

Attached is the quote for the cabling project in the Kennedy Building.

I will see you on Monday at the meeting. If you need anything from me before then, let me know.

We've been experiencing some problems with our photocopier, so the copy may not be too clear. Call me if you can't read it.

Geo

Key to Practice Exercise H

Ralph,

The architects and I have put a schedule together showing the various tasks that need to be accomplished and when. We will be ready to start construction when the rest of the blueprints are turned over to us, which should happen by the end of next week or so. Is that okay with you?

Call me if you want more information on this project. I'll be here most of the rest of the day.

Marge

Quick Reference to Similar Words

Here are sets of commonly misused words, some of which are also contained in Lesson 9: Similar Words and Spelling Tips. The part of speech for each word is indicated by the following key:

adj = adjective

adv = adverb

n = noun

p = pronoun

prep = preposition

v = verb

accept   v: to receive or approve of

except   v: to exclude

Can you *accept* my apology?

Everyone *except* me attended the meeting.

access   v: to have admittance

excess   n: a surplus; adj: extra

You can gain *access* to the funds next week.

We have *excess* cheese and no where to put it.

advice   n: a recommendation (*advice* rhymes with *ice*)

advise   v: to give advice or to make a recommendation

Please give me some *advice* about my paper.

I *advise* you to trust the writing process.

affect	v: to influence
effect	n: result

How will that *affect* you?
The *effect* is not yet known.

a lot	adj: much (sometimes considered colloquial)
alot	not a Standard English spelling

We have *a lot* of issues with that company.

all right	adv: satisfactorily, very well, certainly
	adj: satisfactory, acceptable
alright	not a Standard English spelling

Everything is *all right*, so we can take a short break.

altogether	adv: completely, entirely, wholly
all together	adv: a group that acts or is acted upon collectively

These are *altogether* mine.
The members were *all together* in the board room.

among	prep: together with, along with (more than two)
between	prep: among, together with (when only two are involved)

Between the two of us, who has more time?
Among the three of us, Gerry has more time.

amount	n: quantity, sum, total that cannot be counted individually
number	n: amount or quantity that can be counted individually

A large *number* of people are in the lobby making a huge *amount* of noise.

assure	v: to give someone confidence (the object is a person)
ensure	v: to make certain (the object would be a "thing")
insure	v: to protect against loss

I *assure* you (give you confidence) that nothing will go wrong.

I want to *ensure* (make certain) that nothing goes wrong.

I need to *insure* (protect against loss) this ring.

adverse	adj: unfavorable, bad
averse	adj: reluctant, unenthusiastic

If you have an *adverse* reaction, get help immediately.

If you are *averse* to going to dinner, don't go.

appraise	v: to assess
apprise	v: to inform

Before you *appraise* the situation, speak to Denise.

She will *apprise* you of the latest developments.

are	v: part of the verb *to be* (is, are, was, were)
hour	n: an amount of time
our	p: possessive pronoun for *we*

What *are our* options? We have an *hour* to decide.

brake	n: a stopping device
break	v: to split apart

Put the *brakes* on that deal or it will *break* up our company.

bridal	adj: pertaining to brides
bridle	v: control, rein in, restrain

The *bridal* shower is on Sunday.

We need to *bridle* our spending.

broach	v: to raise a subject
brooch	n: a piece of jewelry

The president *broached* the subject rather gingerly.

Your *brooch* complements your jacket beautifully.

buy	v: to purchase
by	prep: near
bye	interjection: farewell as in *good bye*

Buy the outfit over there *by* the sale items.

I need to tell you *bye* until next week.

cannon	n: a gun
canon	n: body of law

The Civil War *cannon* was on display.

That *canon* explains how to solve my problem.

canvas	n: a type of rough cloth
canvass	v: to examine thoroughly

I made a *canvas* table cloth.
We need to *canvass* the area to determine potential clients.

capital	n: assets, money
	adj: most important
capitol	n: center of government

Our corporation is making a *capital* investment in that city.
When I visit our *capitol*, I intend to go to the Smithsonian.

coarse	adj: rough
course	n: path of travel

Use *coarse* pepper for this recipe.
I'm not sure what *course* we will follow.

censor	v: to cut, edit, or suppress "unacceptable" parts
censure	v: to criticize, show disapproval, or find fault

Sonny *censured* his department for not following policy.
Parts of the movie were *censored* for young viewers.

complacent	adj: self-satisfied
complaisant	adj: willingness to please

Micha had a *complacent* look after the deal.
Silva's *complaisant* attitude is perfect for this job.

complement	n: something that completes
compliment	n: praise, flattering remark
	v: to flatter

She *complimented* him on his suit and tie.
Your scarf *complements* your outfit.

continual	adj: happening frequently with intervals between
continuous	adj: without interruption

The woman's *continuous* talking annoyed everyone.
The buses run on a *continual* basis throughout the night.

core	n: center, nucleus, focal point
corps	n: body, group, unit

Integrity is at the *core* of our values.
The Marine *Corps* has a code of honor.

could of	These spellings are based on colloquial pronunciation;
should of	use *could have* and *should have*.

council	n: a group of leaders
counsel	n: advisor, such as an attorney
	v: advise, guidance

The student *council* has authority over the dress code.
Seek professional *counsel* so that you reduce liability.

desert	n: arid region
	v: abandon
dessert	n: after dinner treat

The *desert* blooms in wintertime.

Pass up *dessert* whenever you have the will.

device	n: tool, gadget, method
devise	v: plan, develop, create

Your *device* should be patented.

When you *devise* a plan, let me know.

elicit	v: to draw out
illicit	adj: unlawful

We can *elicit* a response by offering them a contract.

Illicit behavior in the workplace can lead to a law suit.

elude	v: to escape from
illude	v: to deceive; to mock; to raise hopes and then disappoint.

The answer *eluded* me for some time.

At times, a "bait and switch" tactic *illudes* even astute buyers.

everyday	adj: ordinary or daily
every day	each day: *every* modifies *day*; if you can insert "single" between *every* and *day*, it is two words.

That is an *everyday* routine.

We do that procedure *every day*.

farther	adv: to a greater distance that can be measured: tangible distance
further	adv: to a greater degree or extent: intangible degree

She lives *farther* from work than you do.

Let's discuss this proposal *further*.

faux	adj: fake
foe	n: enemy

In some ways, even *faux* fur hurts animal rights.

Recognize your *foe* early so that you do not lose ground.

gaff	n: a barbed spear
gaffe	n: a mistake

In the Medieval re-enactment, the soldier carried a *gaff*.

Everyone noticed the speaker's *gaffe*.

heal	v: to cure
heel	n: the hind part of foot

To *heal* from your injury, you must rest.

The *heel* of my foot was hurt badly and was bleeding.

hoard	v: to save, stockpile, collect, or squirrel away
horde	n: a crowd, mass, or large group

Many people begin to *hoard* without realizing the consequences.

A *horde* of people awaited the verdict.

its	p: possessive pronoun of *it*
it's	p/v: the contraction for *it is* or *it has*
its'	not a Standard English form: avoid using this construction

The building lost *its* appeal after the crime.

It's a good idea to plan for the future.

It's been a productive day for all of us.

lacks	v: deficient in, short of
lax	adj: loose discipline

The young girl *lacks* nothing but wants everything.

Her behavior might be a result of *lax* parenting.

loose	adj: not tight
lose	v: to misplace or to be defeated

You will feel more comfortable wearing *loose* clothing.

Did you *lose* the game?

may be	v: to suggest possibility
maybe	adv: perhaps

He *may be* the next mayor. *Maybe* it will rain tomorrow.

miner	n: one who mines
minor	adj: small

Both of my grandfathers were *miners*.

That problem is *minor* compared to others.

passed	v: past tense of *to pass*: approved, accepted
past	n: earlier period, previous
	adj: earlier, bygone
	adv: passing or going beyond something

Jon jogged *past* the diner. As he *passed* it, he saw his friend. In the *past*, he wouldn't have stopped.

personal	adj: individual, private
personnel	n: employees; an administrative division of an organization.
	adj: employee issues

Try not to let *personal* problems affect your work.
There are many *personnel* issues to discuss at our meeting.
All *personnel* are required to attend the meeting.

rain	n: precipitation, rainfall
reign	n: time in power, sovereignty
	v: to have control, rule, or influence
rein	v: to curb, restrain, or control

The sound of *rain* is relaxing.
The CEO *reigns* like a king, but his *reign* will soon be over.
If he would *rein* in his power, everyone would be happier.

review	n: a critical report
	v: to examine, appraise
revue	n: theatrical sketches

Be prepared for your annual *review* next week.
When in New York, we went to a comedy *revue*.

sight	n: vision, mental perception
site	n: a location
cite	v: to quote, to name

The *sight* was impaired due to the accident.

My Web *site* is under construction.

I was *cited* for driving without my license.

sometime	adj/adv: an unspecified time
some time	a period of time: *some* modifies *time*; to check if it should be written as one word or two words, remove "some." If your sentence still makes sense, represent it as two words.

He said he would call me *sometime* next week.

We plan to spend *some time* on this before it is complete.

Check: We plan to spend *time* on this before it is complete.

stationary	adj: not moving
stationery	n: writing paper

A *stationary* bicycle is a good type of exercise equipment.

Our company needs new *stationery* because our logo has changed.

than	a conjunction used in comparisons
then	adv: referring to time, as in "after that" or "next"

I would rather get up early *than* sleep late.

When you agree, *then* I will have more time.

their	p: possessive form of *they*
there	adv: in or at "that" place
	p: an anticipating subject
they're	the contracted form of *they are*

Their apartment is next to mine.
There are a lot of people in the lobby.
They're standing next to the reception desk.

themselves	p: the reflexive form of *they*
theirselves	not a Standard English form

They put *themselves* in a precarious position.

to	prep: toward, in the direction of
too	adv: also, besides, very, or excessively

If you go *to* the club, call me *to* tell me what transpired.
We have *too* much information and *too* little time.

through	prep: by means of, from beginning to end, because of
threw	v: past participle of *throw*
thorough	adj: carried through to completion
thru	not a Standard English spelling; use only with "drive-thru"

Walk *through* the room quietly.
Jenkins *threw* the paper at the judge.
We all did a *thorough* job on the report.

vain	adj: ineffective, hopeless, worthless
vane	n: weather vane
vein	n: blood vessel

In my *vain* attempt to help, I created a bigger problem.

The weather *vane* on my house creaks.

The nurse looked for a good *vein* in *vain*.

ware	n: merchandise
wear	v: to be dressed in
where	adv: a place

The vendor's *wares* were out of date.

If you *wear* your best, you will feel confident.

Where did you say you were going?

were	v: past tense form of *to be*
we're	p/v: contraction for *we are*

Were you aware of the issue?

We're going to address it at our next meeting.

who's	p/v: contraction for *who is*
whose	p: possessive pronoun of *who*

Who's going to the party?

Whose book is on the table?

you	a personal pronoun
yous	a colloquial plural form of *you* used in the North and East
y'all	a colloquial plural form of *you* used in the South
you'uns	a colloquial plural form of *you* used in the Midwest

You all should go to the game this Friday.

you're	p/v: contraction for *you are*
your	p: possessive pronoun of *you*

You are more capable than you realize.

You're the best at what you do.

Your way of thinking brightens the room.

Keys to Assessments and Worksheets

LESSON 1

Pre-Assessment
Part A. Punctuation: Commas and Semicolons
1. When you arrive in Tampa, call our district manager.
2. Reserve March 15, 2009, for our reception.
3. Boston, Massachusetts, is a great city for a conference.
4. McKenzie will manage the project; however, Bill will help.
5. As you go through life, always attempt to solve problems in a positive way.
6. No one has all the answers, but everyone has something to contribute.
7. Your presentation will be a success; you know your topic well.
8. However, you should still practice until you feel confident.
9. Martha, thank you for giving me that advice.
10. I will help you with your plans, if you wish.
11. Although I worked hard on the project, I do not feel good about it.
12. My boss, however, said that it turned out well.
13. The time to act is now; therefore, give the interview your best.
14. They will make you the offer; you have nothing to fear.
15. Bob, my associate, will be joining us for dinner.

Part B. Capitalization, Quotation Marks, and Apostrophes
Last week **I** applied for a job and had to go to an **employment interview**. I was applying for a **manager's** position at a local restaurant. When **I** arrived, the **assistant manager** asked me, **"Do** you live in the community?" Since **I** don't live nearby, **I** immediately thought that I would be out of the running for the position. I answered with a cheerful voice, **"No**, but I have access to good transportation.**"** Before I left, the **owner** needed to make a copy of my **driver's** license. Since my resume was missing my previous **employer's** contact information, I said I would call back with the information.

Part C. Similar Words
1. The **principal** and interest on your loan are due.
2. If the problem does not **affect** you, don't worry about it.
3. **Assure** your manager that you will be on time.
4. The **effect** is not yet known.
5. Joe said that he would **lend** you his book.
6. The vehicle lost **its** wheels.
7. All members of the committee should bring **their** reports.
8. When you say **it's** time to send in the report, we will.
9. **They're** working hard to solve the problem.
10. We all try to live by our **principles**.

Part D. Number Usage
1. Kenny ordered **12** notebooks, not **5**.
2. Are you available on September **10** for a meeting?
3. Jackson's current address is 1355 **East** Archer.
4. When you say **thousands** of people will be there, do you mean it?
5. The company sold **$2.5 million** in products.

LESSON 2

Worksheet 1: Identifying Simple Subjects and Verbs
1. Margaret prefers to assist me on this project.
2. The order contained too many unnecessary products.
3. I thanked the new engineer for fixing the electrical problem.
4. (I) Thank you for asking that question.
5. Our new program will begin in one month.
6. Mr. Jarris spoke about the plan in detail at our last meeting.
7. (You) Examine the order carefully before sending it out.
8. My assistant gave me the information on Monday.
9. (You) See the director before you leave today.
10. I am pleased that you are able to join our staff.
11. My new class in business management begins next month.
12. Your response is needed by the director immediately.
13. Will you be able to give the director your response today?
14. (You) Please thank the participants for sharing valuable information with us.
15. Do you have an account at the First National Bank?
16. Our new bank offers great promotional items for its customers.
17. Joseph Campbell encouraged people to find their bliss in life.
18 What are you doing to improving your life's journey?

Worksheet 2: Identifying Compound Subjects and Compound Verbs
1. Juan and Marissa attended the meeting and participated in the discussion.
2. (You) Identify and eliminate excess information in your paper.
3. You and your teammate should prepare the report and present it to the committee.
4. Martin and Silvia rejected the offer and suggested new negations.
5. Your sister or cousin can encourage you and provide you with support.
6. Your interests and hobbies contribute to your profile but do not count for experience.
7. (You) Compose a new resume and include three references.
8. (You) Contact your references and ask for permission to list them on your resume.
9. Giorg and I will host the event and appreciate your attendance.
10. Bankers and brokers have exciting jobs but need to put in long hours.

Worksheet 3: Identifying Subjects and Verbs in Compound Sentences

1. (<u>You</u>) <u>Thank</u> the participants, and let them know how to find the resources.
2. Our <u>instructions</u> <u>were</u> not clear, but our <u>task</u> <u>was completed</u> successfully.
3. <u>Jeremy</u> <u>started</u> his own landscaping business, and <u>he</u> <u>is</u> quite busy now.
4. (<u>You</u>) <u>Call</u> him to see if he needs help, and <u>you</u> <u>might have</u> a part-time job.
5. (<u>You</u>) <u>Tell</u> him about your previous experience, or <u>he</u> <u>may</u> not <u>realize</u> your qualifications.
6. (I) <u>Thank</u> you for getting the project to me early, for <u>I</u> <u>was</u> in a serious time crunch.
7. Some <u>resumes</u> <u>include</u> too much information, so <u>we</u> <u>take</u> that into consideration.
8. (<u>You</u>) <u>Identify</u> your interests, and (<u>You</u>) <u>find</u> time to build them into your schedule.
9. Your <u>skills</u> <u>will help</u> you to get the job, and your <u>attitude</u> <u>will ensure</u> your success.
10. (<u>You</u>) <u>Mark</u> your calendar for April 15, and (<u>You</u>) <u>attend</u> this event with a friend.

LESSON 3

Worksheet 1: Identifying Conjunctions

1. *Although* we were asked to join the group, we declined their invitation. SC
2. Marcus helped us with our plans; *however*, he was not in town for the celebration. AC
3. The new manager implemented the policy, *and* she asked the each of us follow it. CC
4. *While* our company does not have paid leave, it is generous with bonuses. SC
5. (You) Feel free, *therefore*, to submit your resume on line anytime before the 6th of September. AC
6. *Consequently*, we were not able to assist George with his plans. AC
7. I invited their department to the meeting, *but* they had other plans. CC
8. Dr. Martin requested the instructions, *yet* she did not follow them. CC
9. The group will meet in Boston; *therefore*, everyone will find the location convenient. AC
10. Please fill out the form, *and* return it at your convenience. CC

Worksheet 2: Knowing Conjunctions

Coordinating conjunctions: and, but, or, for, nor, so, yet
Subordinating conjunctions: although, because, while, if, as, as soon as
Adverbial conjunctions: however, therefore, for example, consequently

Key Ideas

1. Coordinating conjunctions connect *equal* grammatical parts.
2. Subordinating conjunctions show relationships between ideas and, in the process, make one idea *dependent* on the other.
3. Adverbial conjunctions build bridges between ideas of equal importance: they are known as *transition* words.

Worksheet 3: Identifying Sentences and Fragments.

__F__ 1.   While George and I went to the store last week to buy some office supplies.

__S__ 2.   George suggested that we go to the new store located in the mall.

__F__ 3.   Since it was a holiday, getting there early to find parking nearby without walking a mile.

__S__ 4.   The new office supply store had everything that we needed and more.

__F__ 5.   Of course, adding a few items such as a stapler that weren't on my list.

__S__ 6.   Adding all these extra things to the shopping cart irritated George.

__S__ 7.   Though we are still friends, we may never go shopping together again.

__S__ 8.   Shopping for office supplies is something that I prefer to do alone anyway.

__F__ 9.   When you go shopping with someone like George who doesn't like to shop.

__F__ 10.   Making a list is a good idea, though.

__S__ 11.   When you buy things that aren't on your list, watch out so that you don't make compulsive choices.

__F__ 12.   Items that you don't need or won't use and that create clutter.

__S__ 13.   Some items look appealing at the moment but are useless in the long-run.

__F__ 14.   A professional shopper who knows what to buy and who doesn't end up with things just because they are good deals.

__S__ 15.   The next time that you go shopping, make a list and go with someone who is patient.

LESSON 4

Worksheet 1: Practice for the following comma rules: Conjunction (CONJ), Series (SER), Direct Address (DA)

1.   I <u>completed</u> my report, and <u>Alice</u> <u>sent</u> it to Wanda. CONJ
2.   <u>Wanda</u> <u>received</u> the report, but <u>she</u> <u>did</u> not yet <u>file</u> it with the department. CONJ
3.   (<u>I</u>) <u>Thank</u> you for letting me know about your concern, Marsha. DA
4.   <u>Wanda</u> <u>will appreciate</u> your telling her about the missing information for John Wilson, Bill Jones, and Mark Kramer. SER
5.   (<u>You</u>) <u>Give</u> Wanda the information today, and <u>you</u> <u>will save</u> her some time. CONJ
6.   The <u>report</u> often <u>needs</u> to be adjusted, and <u>Wanda</u> kindly <u>helps</u> us with it. CONJ
7.   Marsha, <u>you</u> <u>are</u> wonderful to assist us with the extra work in our department. DA
8.   <u>You</u> <u>should</u> first <u>work</u> on the monthly report schedules and inventory. No comma
9.   <u>You</u> <u>can ask</u> for additional time, but you may not receive it. CONJ
10.   The training <u>room</u> <u>needs</u> new chairs, tables, and flip charts. SER
11.   (<u>You</u>) <u>Go</u> to the mail room to get the catalog for ordering supplies, Mallory. DA

12. The <u>accounting department</u> <u>issues</u> guidelines for expenses, and <u>someone</u> in that department <u>can assist</u> you with your expense account. CONJ
13. Client <u>lunches</u> <u>are included,</u> but <u>you</u> <u>cannot get</u> reimbursed for meals with friends, family, and co-workers. CONJ, SER
14. (<u>You</u>) <u>File</u> your expense account by the 15th of each month, and <u>you</u> <u>will receive</u> your check by the 30th of the month. CONJ
15. Jorge, (I) <u>thank</u> you for following the policy as it is written. DA

Worksheet 2: Practice for the following comma rules: Introductory (INTRO), Appositive (AP), Direct Address (DA)

1. While <u>I</u> <u>waited</u> for a bus, <u>I</u> <u>was able</u> to complete the report. INTRO
2. However, the <u>report</u> <u>may need</u> some major revisions. INTRO
3. (<u>You</u>) <u>Give</u> me your honest opinion, Mike. DA
4. <u>Mr. Sisco,</u> our new office manager, <u>will use</u> the report to make important decisions. AP
5. If <u>I</u> <u>had known</u> how important the report would be, <u>I</u> <u>would</u> not <u>have</u> <u>agreed</u> to do it. INTRO
6. However, <u>I</u> <u>felt</u> pressured to agree to do it because everyone has too much work. INTRO
7. <u>You</u> <u>can ask</u> Susan, our sales representative, for a second opinion. AP
8. When <u>I</u> <u>started</u> this job, <u>I</u> <u>had</u> no idea about the long work hours. INTRO
9. However, <u>I</u> <u>would have taken</u> it anyway because of its wonderful opportunities. INTRO
10. After <u>you</u> <u>work</u> here for a while, <u>you</u> <u>will appreciate</u> your fellow workers. INTRO
11. Mitchell, <u>could</u> <u>you</u> <u>help</u> George with the new project? DA
12. If <u>you</u> <u>cannot help</u> George at this time, <u>you</u> <u>should</u>n't <u>worry</u> about it. INTRO
13. However, (<u>You</u>) <u>check</u> back with him periodically to see how the project is going. INTRO
14. Our new <u>vice president,</u> Melissa Lorenz, <u>scheduled</u> a meeting for this Friday afternoon. AP
15. Jamie, (<u>You</u>) <u>check</u> with Melissa to find out if the entire department needs to attend. DA

Worksheet 3: Practice for the following comma rules: Conjunction (CONJ), Addresses and Dates (AD), Nonrestrictive (NR) , Parenthetical (PAR)

1. <u>Mr. Gates</u> <u>started</u> a computer company, and <u>Miller</u> <u>decided</u> to invest in it. CONJ
2. <u>Miller,</u> however, <u>did</u> not <u>realize</u> the potential at that time. PAR
3. The <u>company,</u> which is quite successful, <u>has</u> satellites around the world. NR
4. <u>He</u> <u>revealed</u> that March 27, 2008, will be the official kick-off date. AD
5. (<u>You</u>) <u>Arrive</u> to the interview on time, and <u>you</u> <u>will get</u> off to a good start. CONJ
6. <u>We</u> <u>have,</u> as a result, <u>chosen</u> another vendor. PAR
7. The time management <u>seminar</u> <u>was</u> excellent, and its <u>cost</u> <u>was</u> reasonable. CONJ
8. Your <u>paper,</u> unfortunately, <u>did</u> not <u>meet</u> the standards. PAR
9. Our management <u>team</u> <u>assessed</u> the damages, and <u>they</u> <u>recommended</u> changes. CONJ
10. On September 5, 2008, <u>we</u> <u>will arrive</u> in Denver Colorado for a meeting. AD

11. <u>Leadership</u> <u>is</u> a vital topic, but <u>no one</u> <u>seems</u> to be addressing it. CONJ
12. <u>Simone</u> <u>will,</u> however, <u>assist</u> you with the project. PAR

Worksheet 4: Practice for the following comma rules: Introductory (INTRO), Series (SER), Words Omitted (WO), Contrasting Expression or Afterthought (CEA)
1. If <u>you</u> <u>choose</u> to attend the event, <u>(You)</u> <u>let</u> us know by the end of the day. INTRO
2. <u>(You)</u> <u>Bring</u> a guest to the luncheon, if you prefer. CEA
3. If <u>you</u> <u>need</u> extra tickets, <u>(you)</u> <u>ask</u> Elizabeth. INTRO
4. After the awards, <u>they</u> <u>will serve</u> a meal of fish potatoes and broccoli. INTRO
5. <u>(You)</u> <u>Resume</u> the program at the north branch, not at the south branch. CEA
6. Although the <u>offer</u> still <u>stands,</u> our <u>deadline</u> quickly <u>approaches</u>. INTRO
7. Before <u>they</u> <u>rescind</u> their offer, <u>(You)</u> <u>give</u> them an answer. INTRO
8. After <u>you</u> <u>review</u> the contract, <u>(You)</u> <u>let</u> us know what you think. INTRO
9. The <u>contract</u> <u>can be changed,</u> but only on our terms. CEA
10. Your <u>feedback</u> <u>should include</u> items to add, delete, or change. SER
11. The <u>fact</u> <u>is,</u> your input will assist us in many ways. WO
12. <u>(You)</u> <u>Begin</u> the year with a detailed, comprehensive plan. WO

LESSON 5

Worksheet 1. Semicolon No Conjunction (NC) and Comma Conjunction (CONJ)
1. The Green Tree <u>reception</u> <u>was</u> elegant; <u>it</u> <u>was</u> a black tie event. NC
2. I <u>arrived</u> early to the event, and <u>everyone</u> <u>seemed</u> very friendly. CONJ
3. The <u>group</u> <u>expressed</u> concern about the environment; <u>they</u> all <u>wanted</u> to see immediate and substantial change. NC
4. The keynote <u>speaker</u> <u>shared</u> new data about climate change; <u>everyone</u> <u>listened</u> attentively to the entire speech. NC
5. <u>Mark</u> <u>suggested</u> that we join the group, so <u>he</u> <u>inquired</u> about the requirements for membership. CONJ
6. <u>Membership</u> <u>required</u> participation at various levels; <u>both</u> of us <u>were</u> already overextended. NC
7. The group's <u>mission</u> <u>appealed</u> to me, and I was excited about getting involved. CONJ
8. <u>Mark</u> <u>thought</u> it over for a while, yet <u>he</u> <u>was</u> still not ready to commit. CONJ
9. The environmental <u>movement</u> <u>grows</u> every year, but more <u>help</u> <u>is</u> urgently <u>needed</u>. CONJ
10. <u>Mark</u> finally <u>agreed</u> to join the group; my <u>excitement</u> <u>tipped</u> him in the right direction. NC
11. Their first <u>meeting</u> <u>is</u> next week, and <u>we</u> both <u>plan</u> to go to it. CONJ
12. I <u>will volunteer</u> for the same project that Mark works on; <u>working</u> together <u>is</u> fun. NC

Worksheet 2. Semicolon Bridge (BR) and Comma Parenthetical (PAR)

1. <u>Keeping up with technology</u> <u>can</u>, however, <u>make</u> a difference in your career. PAR
2. Different <u>generations</u> <u>have</u> different sorts of issues with technology; for example, younger <u>people</u> <u>have</u> an easier time learning new technology. BR
3. Today's young <u>people</u> <u>used</u> computers throughout their schooling; consequently, <u>they</u> <u>find</u> technology a natural part of their world. BR
4. Older <u>generations</u>, however, <u>didn't</u> <u>have</u> access to technology in school. PAR
5. <u>They</u> <u>needed</u> to learn how to use computers and software on the job; as a result, <u>many</u> <u>consider</u> themselves "technologically illiterate." BR
6. <u>It</u> <u>is</u> never too late, though, to learn how to use a computer. PAR
7. <u>Taking classes</u> at a local college <u>can</u> sometimes <u>be</u> inconvenient; however, <u>you</u> <u>can research</u> training opportunities online. BR
8. Online <u>classes</u> <u>make</u> learning convenient; for example, <u>you</u> <u>can learn</u> while you are in your own home office. BR
9. Most <u>companies</u> <u>offer</u> in-house training; fortunately, their <u>employees</u> <u>stay</u> at the cutting edge of technology. BR
10. <u>Getting a job</u> at a major corporation, therefore, <u>helps ensure</u> that you will keep your skills up-to-date. PAR
11. (<u>You</u>) <u>Take</u> advantage of all opportunities to build your skills; for example, (<u>you</u>) <u>keep</u> an eye on your college and company newsletters. BR
12. Computer <u>classes</u> and other sorts of career <u>classes</u> <u>are offered</u>; however, only the most <u>motivated</u> <u>enroll</u> in them. BR

Worksheet 3. Semicolon and Comma Review

1. <u>Finding a job</u> <u>is</u> challenging; however, certain <u>pointers</u> <u>can help</u> <u>make</u> it easier. BR
2. <u>You</u> <u>need</u> to stay abreast of job search techniques; fortunately, <u>best practices</u> <u>are</u> easily accessible. BR
3. <u>You</u> <u>must do</u> your research; college placement offices, online sources, and books provide an abundance of information. NC, SER
4. A <u>colleague</u> of mine <u>applied</u> for jobs in such diverse locations as Buffalo, New York; Oak Brook, Illinois; and Phoenix Arizona. BC
5. <u>Searching</u> for a job online <u>expedited</u> the project; however, the <u>job</u> <u>search</u> <u>was</u> still demanding and taxing. BR
6. Most <u>people</u> <u>don't</u> <u>like</u> extended periods of not knowing where their future lies; <u>facing the unknown</u> <u>creates</u> anxiety. NC
7. <u>Staying busy</u> <u>is</u> a key to managing a job search; the more (that) you do, the better (that) you will feel about yourself and your opportunities. BC
8. (<u>You</u>) <u>Spend</u> as much time as you can on your job search; in fact, some <u>people</u> <u>say</u> that you need to treat "finding a job as a full-time a job." BR
9. (<u>You</u>) <u>Print</u> a business card that gives your contact information; (<u>You</u>) <u>update</u> your resume. NC
10. (<u>You</u>) <u>Consider</u> networking as one of your primary sources for leads; therefore, (<u>you</u>) <u>make</u> a list of people whom you can contact and events that you can attend. BR
11. (<u>You</u>) <u>Stay</u> positive about your future; <u>something</u> good <u>will happen</u> when you least expect it. NC

12. <u>Securing your dream job</u> <u>is</u> not an end to the process in today's world; <u>business changes</u> constantly. NC
13. <u>Doing a great job</u> <u>does</u> not <u>ensure</u> that you will stay with a company forever; <u>keeping your skills up-to-date</u> <u>is</u> your best insurance for a secure future. NC
14. (<u>You</u>) <u>Keep</u> your finances flexible; (<u>You</u>) <u>save</u> regularly so that you have a nest egg to finance your next job search. NC
15. With hard work and a little luck, <u>you</u> <u>will achieve</u> your dreams; <u>you</u> <u>deserve</u> the best! INTRO, NC

LESSON 6

Worksheet 1. Colons and Dashes
Note: The answers may vary as colons and dashes are somewhat interchangeable.
1. Jeremy suggested several changes—add more personnel, start offering carry out, and remain open on Sundays—but I disagree with him on all points.
2. Here's what you need to look out for: their Eastern branch office does not have a sales manager.
3. If you ask for a lower price—even one that is not unreasonable—they will not know how to handle your request.
4. Caution: Do not use this equipment in temperatures below freezing.
5. Note: Friday is a holiday and our offices will be closed.
6. Sean refused to share the plan: he simple wouldn't answer my questions. (Note: A dash would also work.)
7. These are the people you should interview: Eddie Stone, Fred Harris, and Bill Janulewicz. (Note: A dash could also be correct.)
8. All of them—especially Bill Janulewicz—are extremely knowledgeable of our products.
9. Remain positive: you do not yet know how they will respond to your offer. (Note: A dash could also be correct.)
10. I received a call from McCracken's CEO—yes, their CEO—to join the marketing team.

Worksheet 2. Colons, Dashes, and Ellipses
Note: The colon and dash are often interchangeable; answers may vary.
1. Scot said that we shouldn't worry . . . the product research team will meet tomorrow.
2. Note: The following, more people need to travel today but fewer people enjoy it.
3. The Mercer group became involved of their own accord—I didn't invite them. (Note: A colon or even a semicolon would also be correct.)
4. Follow your passions: you will create a career that you enjoy.
5. I couldn't understand what John said, "The biggest seller is . . . ."
6. Send your resume directly to the CEO—he is expecting to hear from you.
7. Toni and Joe bought the company—they are ecstatic.

8. You know what I mean—things just aren't working out. Or: You know what I mean . . . things just aren't working out.
9. Keep your spirits up—you will have another opportunity soon.
10. Read between the lines . . . watch the body language.

LESSON 7

Worksheet 1. Capitalization and Number Usage

Dear Suzie,

Thank you for asking for more information about my work history. For five years, I worked for Rapid Communications as an associate manager in the Customer Service Department. Here's information about how to contact my former boss, Jake Roberts, human resources director:

Mr. Jake Roberts
Human Resources Director
Rapid Communications
14 North Ogden Road
Burlington, IA 52601

I look forward to hearing from you. You can reach me at 209-555-1212 anytime between 9 a.m. and 5 p.m. Monday through Friday until the end of August.

Best regards,

Sylvia Marina

Worksheet 2. Number Usage and Capitalization
1. The supply company delivered five copiers and seven fax machines.
2. Ian, our new company auditor, scheduled the meeting for Friday, September 10 at 9 a.m.
3. Send the information to Lester Ostrom, 1213 West Astor Place, Chicago, IL 60610.
4. Did you request 12 catalogs or only 2?
5. The new budget for our computer purchase is $1.5 million.
6. We received hundreds of calls, not thousands as Jeffrey said.
7. Did you say I should meet you for lunch today at 12 o'clock (or 12 noon or 12 p.m.) or on Monday?
8. Austin Roberts, accounting manager, gave me the instructions on how to complete my taxes.
9. Vice President Tomas O'Rourke has a background in law.
10. If the requirements call for five postings on three different days, allow yourself at least two hours a day to get the work done.

11. We had a 10 percent decrease in our heating bill but a 50 percent increase in water.
12. The closet is 5 feet by eight feet.
13. If I can assist you with one-half of the mailing, let me know.
14. Eleven of the participants have arrived, but the remaining twelve are late.
15. Meet me on the fourteenth floor at 3:30 this afternoon. (Or: at 3:30 p.m.)

Worksheet 3. Review: Punctuation, Capitalization, and Number Usage

1. Many colleges are offering online degrees, and you should learn more about the opportunities you have for finishing your degree. CONJ
2. Do your research: only attend a fully accredited online college or university.
3. If one-half or more of the course offerings are online, the college's commitment to online learning is strong.
4. A friend of mine received her doctorate online; as a result, she increased her income and her job opportunities. BR
5. A decade ago, few colleges offered classes online; now hundreds of colleges and universities offer classes online. INTRO
6. Some of the advantages of online learning include the following: you can attend classes in the comfort of your own home, you can make use of special support services and tutorials, and you can learn at your own pace. SER
7. Online learning occurs in countries around the world, and thousands of students learn in virtual classrooms every day. CONJ
8. Though class size varies, many classes limit the number of participants to twenty students. INTRO
9. One of the results of online learning is improved writing skills; good writing skills will benefit you throughout your career. NC
10. Finishing your education is what's important: get your degree online or attend college at a local university. (Note: a semicolon or dash would also be correct.)

LESSON 8

Worksheet 1. Quotations, Apostrophes, and Hyphens

1. Margaret's report is a first-class example of what we need.
2. Bob asked, "May I receive a copy of the Barker proposal?"
3. If you can prove "that dog can hunt," we'll sign on to the "dotted line."
4. A one-day workshop would help our part-time staff.
5. After I rejected their "proposal," Mel's response was "great."
6. What's next on the agenda for our mid-week meeting?
7. When I said "the game's over," I was referring to Bill's role.
8. A full-time position is open in our accounting department.
9. A month's worth of invoices are sitting on my desk.
10. You can use Jan's office until the first-floor conference room is free.

Worksheet 2. Review of Commas, Semicolons, Apostrophes, and Hyphens

1. Our broker's message got lost in the shuffle, so I had to find his number on the Internet. CONJ
2. When I use the term "fixin' to," it means that I'm ready to go do something.
3. Do you have any favorite colloquial terms, Sasha?
4. Call to see if their account executive is available; if not, don't leave a message. BR (or NC and INTRO)
5. Let's go to the second-hand shop to pick up supplies for our camping trip.
6. Mandy, my new sales representative called about our "delay." DA
7. The short- and long-terms projections will be available after 3 p.m. today.
8. It's been a long day already, and one-half of my work is yet to be done. CONJ
9. Enclose your check in the postage-paid envelope, and send it to us by Friday. CONJ
10. Sandro's half-baked idea was a hit at our department's meeting.

LESSON 9

Worksheet 1. Similar Words

1. They have *too* many new projects and *too* little time.
2. You will be *apprised* of the situation before noon today.
3. Jackson *assured* me that you got the job.
4. If you feel *all right* about it, ask for a raise.
5. *You're* the right person to turn the situation around.
6. *Among* the three of us, we have all the resources we need.
7. Try *to* see Leonard before you leave today.
8. Kevin said that he would *lend* me his notes.
9. His remark was a real *compliment*.
10. I live *farther* from work *than* you do.
11. If you *could have* spoken to Della, you'd understand.
12. Vera *passed* that trait on to her daughters *too*.
13. How will that *affect* you?
14. When you know the *effect*, let me know.
15. Carol *lent* me everything I needed for the trip.
16. The project lost *its* appeal after Mike quit.
17. I *ensure* all print materials will be of high quality.
18. After you *assure* me, *assure* the others also.
19. *Their* boat has left the dock.
20. We are *further* along *than* we realize.
21. Say *it's* time to go, and we will.
22. If the bank will *lend* you enough funds, will you buy the car?
23. My *principal* and interest are due on the 1st of the month.
23. That company does all training on *site*.
24. Did the officer *cite* you for the violation?
25. We all try to live by our *principles*.

Worksheet 2. Similar Words
Answers will vary.

1. its   The car lost its appeal after I learned its price.
2. their   You can see their car through the window.
3. than   If you have more time than I do, help me on the project.
4. adverse   I had an adverse reaction to the medication.
5. too   If you have too little time, don't help me on the project.
6. assure   If you assure me that the work will be done, I will wait for it.
7. it's   When you say it's been a challenge, what do you mean?
8. effect   They insisted the effect was due to our negligence.
9. loan   You can get a loan at your local bank.
10. further   The further you stray from the subject, the longer this will take.
11. they're   They're not interested in the details.
12. ensure   Brandon ensured the quality of the work.
13. affect   The decision will affect everyone involved.
14. then   Do your work then go to the store.
15. all right If it's all right with you, let's not have lunch today.
16. doesn't   Margaret doesn't agree with me either.
17. don't   The decision makers don't have an answer.
18. saw   Jimmy saw the movie last week.
19. seen   I have not seen it, though.
20. principle That is a good principle to live by.

LESSON 10

Key to Post-Assessment
Part A. Punctuation: Commas and Semicolons

1. When Jason presents his information, assist him with the handouts.

2. Plan to attend the meeting on Wednesday, April 15, at 9 o'clock.

3. Chicago, Illinois, is the location we have chosen for our conference.

4. I will make the arrangements for our retreat; however, Miller will help.

5. When things don't go as you planned, keep an open mind.

6. Everyone would like to get the promotion, but it can only go to one person.

7. You will do well in Phoenix; you prepared for everything that could go wrong.

8. However, you should still remain humble until it is over.

9. David, you have been a great support the last few weeks.

10. You can bring a guest with you to the dinner, if you wish.

11. Although Bob helped me on the assignment, I did not do well enough to pass.

12. My professor, however, said that I could repeat it.

13. The opportunity will not present itself again; do your best.

14. You can accept their offer; you will not regret it.

15. Mitchell, my cousin, will be here for lunch today.

Part B. Capitalization, Quotation Marks, and Apostrophes

The **restaurant** that **I** interviewed with finally got back to me. The job that **I** was applying for was a **manager's** position. For the past week or so, **I** have been concerned about some of my **answers** and missing information on my resume. Then I sent the **assistant manager** a note asking him, "**Would** you like for me to send you an updated resume?" Since I had not heard back from him, **I** assumed it was because **I** didn't do well. Every time I felt bad, I said to myself, "**Don't** worry—you gave it your best—no one is perfect." Would you believe it if I told you they offered me the job? Of course, I will accept it—a **manager's** position is exactly what I was hoping to find.

Part C. Similar Words

1. How much do you pay in **principal** and interest?
2. The **effect** of the problem was not yet known.
3. Can you **assure** me that the assignment will be in on time?
4. Bob's decision to hire a new employee will **affect** my job.
5. If you will **lend** me your car, I will take good care of it.
6. My car loses **its** traction on icy roads.
7. When you say **their** reports are late, do mean all reports?
8. If you say **it's** time to renew our membership, we will.
9. Adams asked if **there** are issues that we need to resolve.
10. Live by your **principles**, and you will have fewer regrets.

Part D. Number Usage

1. Alice brought **ten** notebooks, but we needed only **five**.
2. The meeting was held on **November 12** last year.
3. Do you live at 1200 **West** Jarwin?
4. Alyssa has **hundreds** of friends.
5. The contract was worth **$1.5 million**.

Note: You will find additional practice worksheets at the student Web site for this book: www.commasrule.com.

SCORE SHEET

Instructions: From a total possible 100 points, subtract 2 point for each error.

Part A. Punctuation: 40 Possible Points
Part B. Capitalization, Quotation Marks,
      and Apostrophes: 30 Possible Points
Part C. Similar Words: 20 Possible Points
Part D. Number Usage: 10 Possible Points

	Pretest Score	**Posttest Score**	**Difference**	**Percent Improvement**
Part A	_____	_____	_____	_____
Part B	_____	_____	_____	_____
Part C	_____	_____	_____	_____
Part D	_____	_____	_____	_____
Total	_____	_____	_____	_____

To calculate the percent of improvement, divide the difference between the pretest score and the posttest score by the pretest score. For example:

Total	**60**	**80**	**20**	**33%**

Here's a step-by-step formula to calculate your score:

1. Count the number of errors for each part and multiply by 2.
2. Deduct that number from 100 to get your total score.
3. When you have both your pretest and posttest scores, subtract your pretest score from your posttest score to get the difference.
4. Divide the difference by your pretest score to get the percent of improvement.

INDEX

About the Author

Dona Young is a teacher, facilitator, and writing coach. In addition to teaching writing at Indiana University Northwest, she also facilitates writing programs at major corporations.

Young holds a B.A. from Northern Illinois University and an M.A. from The University of Chicago. Young considers herself a lifelong learner, believing that who we become is a result of what we learn. Young is also the author the following books:

Foundations of Business Communication:
An Integrative Approach
McGraw-Hill/Irwin, 2006

Business English:
Writing for the Global Workplace
McGraw-Hill Higher Education, 2008

Which Comes First, the Comma or the Pause:
A Guide to Business Writing
Writer's Toolkit Publishing, 2009

Writing from the Core: A Guide to Writing
Writer's Toolkit Publishing, 2010

Made in United States
Orlando, FL
01 February 2025

58040044R00128